August Crull

Hymn book for the use of Evangelical Lutheran schools and congregations

August Crull

Hymn book for the use of Evangelical Lutheran schools and congregations

ISBN/EAN: 9783742877451

Manufactured in Europe, USA, Canada, Australia, Japa

Cover: Foto ©ninafisch / pixelio.de

Manufactured and distributed by brebook publishing software (www.brebook.com)

August Crull

Hymn book for the use of Evangelical Lutheran schools and congregations

CONTENTS.

		Page
I.	WORSHIP (Nos. 1-9)	1
II.	ADVENT AND CHRISTMAS (10-15)	9
III.	NEW YEAR (16-18)	20
IV.	THE PASSION (19-27)	25
V.	EASTER (28-34)	38
VI.	ASCENSION (35-37)	50
VII.	WHITSUNTIDE (38-41)	53
VIII.	TRINITY (42—44)	59
IX.	REFORMATION (45-47)	63
X.	THE WORD OF GOD AND THE CHURCH (48-52)	66
XI.	THE CATECHISM (53-60)	72

(1. In general; 2. The Ten Commandments; 3. The Creed; 4. Baptism; 5. The Lord's Supper).

XII.	REPENTANCE (61-65).....................	90
XIII.	FAITH AND JUSTIFICATION (66-72).........	98
XIV.	PRAISE TO JESUS (73-78)................	106
XV.	THE CHRISTIAN LIFE (79-83).............	117
XVI.	MORNING (84-86)........................	124
XVII.	EVENING (87-92)	128
XVIII.	PRAISE AND THANKSGIVING (93-101)........	135
XIX.	THE CROSS AND CONSOLATION (102-110).....	140
XX.	DEATH (111-118)........................	163
XXI.	BURIAL (119-124).......................	175
XXII.	JUDGMENT AND ETERNITY (125-130).........	182
	DOXOLOGIES.............................	193

I. Worship.

1

1. ALL glory be to God on High,
Who hath our race befriended!
To us no harm shall now come nigh,
The strife at last is ended;
God showeth His good will to men,
And peace shall reign on earth again;
Oh! thank him for His goodness.

2. We praise, we worship Thee, we trust,
And give Thee thanks for ever,
O FATHER, that Thy rule is just,
And wise, and changes never:
Thy boundless power o'er all things reigns,
Thou dost whate'er Thy will ordains;
Well for us that Thou rulest!

3. O JESUS CHRIST, our God and Lord,
Son of Thy Heavenly Father,
O Thou who hast our peace restored,
And the lost sheep dost gather,
Thou Lamb of God, to Thee on high
From out our depths we sinners cry,
Have mercy on us, Jesus!

WORSHIP.

4. O Holy Ghost, Thou precious Gift,
    Thou Comforter unfailing,
    O'er Satan's snares our souls uplift,
    And let Thy power availing
    Avert our woes and calm our dread:
    For us the Saviours' blood was shed;
    We trust in Thee to save us.
    N. Decius.

2

1. LORD Jesus Christ, be present now!
    And let Thy Holy Spirit bow
    All hearts in love and fear to-day,
    To hear the truth and keep Thy way.

2. Open our lips to sing Thy praise,
    Our hearts in true devotion raise;
    Our faith increase, our minds enlight,
    That we may know Thy name aright:

3. Until we join the host that cry,
    "Holy art Thou, O Lord, most High!"
    And 'mid the light of that blest place
    Shall gaze upon Thee face to face.

4. Glory to God, the Father, Son,
    And Holy Spirit, Three in One!

To Thee, O blessed Trinity,
Be praise throughout eternity!
Wm. August II, Duke of Saxe-Weimar.

3

1. BLESSED Jesus, at Thy word
We are gathered all to hear Thee;
Let our hearts and souls be stirred
Now to seek and love and fear Thee;
By Thy teachings sweet and holy
Drawn from earth to love Thee solely.

2. All our knowledge, sense, and sight
Lie in deepest darkness shrouded,
Til Thy Spirit breaks our night
With the beams of truth unclouded.
Thou alone to God canst win us,
Thou must work all good within us.

3. Glorious Lord, Thyself impart!
Light of light, from God proceeding,
Open Thou our ears and heart,
Help us by Thy Spirit's pleading,
Hear the cry Thy people raises,
Hear, and bless our prayers and praises.

4. Evermore be praise to Thee,
   Father, Son, and Holy Spirit!
   Of Thy gospel's purity,
   Lord, Thy church not disinherit,
   While we here below must wander,
   Till we sing Thy praises yonder.

   T. Clausnitzer.

4.

1. COME, Holy Ghost, in faith us teach
   To love none but our Saviour
   From all our heart, with all our might,
   And thus to serve Him ever,
   That we, 'gainst death, our fiercest foe,
   Find shelter in His wounds, and so
   Be rescued by His merit.

2. Grant that Thy wholesome doctrine's power
   May be our dearest treasure,
   And let Thy word, the bread of life,
   Help us to heaven's pleasure.
   Yea, let us die to every sin,
   Revive the life of faith again,
   To bear fruit of the Spirit

3. When life and breath depart from us
   In death's last awful hour,

Oh! may our hearts then realize
The working of Thy power;
That we into our Saviour's hand
With conscious trust our souls commend,
To gain rest everlasting.

B. Ringwaldt.

5

1. THIS is the day the Lord hath made;
   He calls the hours His own:
   Let heaven rejoice, let earth be glad,
   And praise surround the throne.

2. To-day He rose and left the dead,
   And Satans empire fell;
   To-day the saints His triumph spread,
   And all His wonders tell.

3. Hosanna to the anointed King,
   To David's holy Son;
   Help us, O Lord; descend, and bring
   Salvation from Thy throne.

4. Blest be the Lord, who comes to men
   With messages of grace;
   Who comes in God His Father's name
   To save our sinful race.

5. Hosanna in the highest strains
   The Church on earth can raise;
   The highest heavens in which he reigns
   Shall give Him nobler praise.

   Psalm. 118.—Watts.

6

1. ABIDE among us with Thy grace,
   Lord Jesus, evermore,
   Nor let us e'er to sin give place,
   Nor grieve Him we adore.

2. Abide among us with Thy word,
   Redeemer, whom we love,
   Thy help and mercy here afford,
   And life with Thee above.

3. Abide omong us with Thy ray,
   O Light that lighten'st all,
   And let Thy truth preserve our way,
   Nor suffer us to fall.

4. Abide with us to bless us still,
   O bounteous Lord of peace;
   With grace and power our souls fulfill,
   Our faith and love increase.

5. Abide among us as our shield,
   O Captain of Thy host;
   That to the world we may not yield,
   Nor e'er forsake our post.

6. Abide with us in faithful love,
   Our God and Saviour be,
   Thy help at need, oh, let us prove,
   And keep us true to Thee.

J. Stegman.

7

1. LORD, Thou art the Truth and Way:
   Guide us, lest we go astray.
   Lord, Thou art the Life: by Thee
   May we gain eternity.

2. In ourselves we cannot trust;
   Lord, remember we are dust!
   Thou who all our frailty know'st,
   Send Thou us Thy Holy Ghost!

From the Danish.

8

1. ALMIGHTY God! Thy Word is cast
   Like seed into the ground;
   Now let the dew of Heaven descend,
   And righteous fruits abound.

2. Let not the foe of Christ and man
   This holy seed remove;
   But give it root in every heart,
   To bring forth fruits of love.

3. Let not the world's deceitful cares
   The rising plant destroy;
   But let it yield a hundred fold —
   The fruits of peace and joy.

4. Oft as the precious seed is sown,
   Thy quickening grace bestow,
   That all whose souls the truth receive
   Its saving power may know.
   From J. Cawood

9

1. LORD, dismiss us with thy blessing,
   Fill our hearts with joy and peace!
   Let us each, thy love possessing,
   Triumph in redeeming grace.
     O refresh us,
   Travelling through this wilderness.

2. Thanks we give and adoration
   For Thy Gospel's joyful sound.
   May the fruits of Thy salvation

WORSHIP.

   In our hearts and lives abound:
      May Thy presence
   With us evermore be found.

3. So whene'er the signal's given
   Us from earth to call away,
   Borne on angel's wings to heaven,
   Glad the summons to obey,
      May we, ready,
   Rise and reign in endless day.
W. Shirley.

II. Advent and Christmas.

10.

1. LIFT up your heads, ye mighty gates!
   Behold the King of glory waits;
   The King of Kings is drawing near,
   The Saviour of the world is here;
   Life and salvation He doth bring,
   Wherefore rejoice and gladly sing;
   We praise Thee, Father, now,
   Creator wise art Thou!

2. The Lord is just, a Helper tried,
   Mercy is ever at his side;
   His kingly crown in holiness,
   His sceptre, pity in distress.

The end of all our woe He brings;
Wherefore the earth is glad and sings:
We praise Thee, Saviour, now,
Mighty in deed art Thou!

3. O blest the land, the city blest,
Where Christ the Ruler is confessed!
O happy hearts and happy homes,
To whom this King in triumph comes!
The cloudless Sun of joy He is,
Who bringeth pure delight and bliss:
O Comforter Divine,
What boundless grace is Thine!

4. Fling wide the portals of your heart;
Make it a temple, set apart
From earthly use for heaven's employ,
Adorned with prayer, and love, and joy;
So shall your Sovereign enter in,
And new and nobler life begin:
To Thee, O God, be praise,
For word, and deed, and grace!

5. Redeemer, come! I open wide
My heart to Thee; here, Lord, abide!
Let me Thy inner presence feel,
Thy grace and love in me reveal,

ADVENT AND CHRISTMAS.

Thy Holy Spirit guide us on,
Until our glorious goal be won!
Eternal praise and fame
We offer to thy name.

G. Velssel

11.

1. HAIL to the Lord's Anointed,
   Great David's greater Son!
   Hail, in the time appointed,
   His reign on earth begun!
   He comes to break oppression,
   To set the captive free,
   To take away transgression.
   And rule in equity.

2. He comes with succor speedy
   To those who suffer wrong;
   To help the poor and needy,
   And bid the weak be strong;
   To give them songs for sighing,
   Their darkness turn to light,
   Whose souls, condemned and dying.
   Were precious in His sight.

3. He shall come down like showers
   Upon the fruitful earth;

And love, joy, hope, like flowers,
Spring in His path to birth.
Before him, on the mountains,
Shall peace, the herald, go;
And righteousness, in fountains,
From hill to valley flow.

4. For Him shall prayer unceasing
And daily vows ascend;
His kingdom still increasing,
A kingdom without end.
The tide of time shall never
His covenant remove;
His name shall stand forever,
That name to us is love.

J. Montgomery.

12

1. O LORD, how shall I meet Thee,
How welcome Thee aright?
All nations long to greet Thee,
My hope, my heart's delight!
O kindle, Lord most holy,
Thy lamp within my breast,
To do in spirit lowly
All that may please Thee best.

2. Thy Zion strews before Thee
 Green branches and fair palms,
 And I, too, will adore Thee,
 With sweetest songs and psalms.
 My soul puts off her sadness,
 Thy glories to proclaim;
 With all her strength and gladness
 She fain would serve Thy Name.

3. What hast Thou e'er neglected
 For my good here below?
 When heart and soul dejected
 Were sunk in darkest woe.
 In deepest degradation,
 Devoid of joy and peace:
 Then Thou, my soul's salvation,
 Didst come to bring release.

4. I lay in fetters groaning,
 Thou comest to set me free.
 I stood, my shame bemoaning,
 Thou comest to honor me.
 A glory Thou dost give me,
 A treasure safe on high,
 That will not fail, nor leave me,
 As earthly riches fly.

5. Nought, nought, dear Lord could move Thee
To leave Thy heavenly place,
Save love, for which I love Thee;
A love that could embrace
A world where sorrow dwelleth,
Which sin and suffering fill,
More than the tongue e'er telleth;
Yet Thou couldst love it still!

6. Rejoice then, ye sad-hearted,
Who sit in deepest gloom,
Who mourn o'er joys departed,
And tremble at your doom;
Despair not, He is near you,
Yea standeth at the door,
Who best can help and cheer you,
And bids you weep no more.

7. No care, nor effort either
Is needed day and night,
How ye may draw Him hither
In your own strength and might.
He comes, He comes with gladness,
By pity moved alone,
To soothe all pain and sadness
That unto Him is known.

8. Nor need ye tremble over
The guilt that gives distress;
No! Jesus all will cover
With grace and righteousness.
He comes to heal the spirit
That mourneth, sin-oppressed,
He comes, that we inherit
Eternal joy and rest.

9. Why should the wicked move you?
Why heed their craft and spite?
The Saviour who doth love you
Will scatter all their might.
He comes a conqueror glorious
O'er all His earthly foes;
In vain His course victorious
They struggle to oppose.

10. He comes to judge the nations,
A terror to His foes,
A light of consolations
And blessed hope to those
Who love the Lord's appearing:
O glorious Sun, now come,
Send forth Thy beams so cheering,
And guide us safely home!

P. Gerhardt.

13

1. LET us all with gladsome voice
   Praise the God of heaven,
   Who to bid our hearts rejoice
   His own Son hath given.

2. Down to this sad earth He comes,
   Here to serve us deigning,
   That with Him in yon fair homes
   We may once be reigning.

3. We are rich, for He was poor,
   Gaze upon this wonder!
   Let us praise God evermore,
   Here on earth and yonder.

4. Look on all who sorrow here,
   Lord, in pity bending,
   Grant us now a glad New Year,
   And a blessed ending.

   U. Langhanns.

14

1. FROM heaven above to earth I come
   To bear good news to every home;
   Glad tidings of great joy I bring,
   Whereof I now will say and sing:

2. To you this night is born a child
Of Mary, chosen virgin mild;
This little child of lowly birth
Shall be the joy of all the earth.

3. This is the Christ our God and Lord,
Who in all need will aid afford;
He will Himself your Saviour be,
From all your sins to set you free.

4. To you the blessedness He bears,
Which God the Father's love prepares,
That in His heavenly Kingdom blest,
You may with us forever rest.

5. These are the tokens ye shall mark:
The swaddling clothes and manger dark;
There shall ye find the infant laid,
By whom the heavens and earth were made.

6. Then let us all with gladsome cheer
Follow the shepherds, and draw near
To see this wondrous gift of God,
Who hath His only Son bestowed.

7. Give heed, my heart, lift up thine eyes!
Who is it in yon manger lies!

Who is this child so young and fair!
Dear little Jesus lieth there.

8. Welcome to earth, Thou noble Guest,
Through whom the sinful world is blest!
In my distress Thou comest to me;
What thanks shall I return to Thee!

9. Ah Lord, who hast created all,
How hast Thou made Thee weak and small,
That Thou must lie on coarse dry grass,
The food of humble ox and ass!

10. Were earth a thousand times as fair,
Beset with gold and jewels rare,
She yet were far too poor to be
A narrow cradle, Lord, for Thee.

11. For velvets soft and silken stuff
Thou hast but hay and straw so rough,
Whereon Thou, King, so rich and great,
As't were thy heaven, art throned in state.

12. And thus, dear Lord, it pleaseth Thee
To make this truth quite plain to me,
That all the world's wealth, honor, might
Are nought and worthless in Thy sight.

ADVENT AND CHRISTMAS. 19

13. O, dearest Jesus, holy Child,
    Make Thee a bed, soft, undefiled,
    Within my heart, that it may be
    A quiet chamber kept for Thee.

14. My heart for very joy doth leap,
    My lips no more can silence keep;
    I too must raise with joyful tongue
    That sweetest ancient cradle-song:

15. Glory to God in highest heaven,
    Who unto man His Son hath given!
    For this His hosts, on joyful wing,
    A blest New Year of mercy sing.

                                    M. Luther.

15

1. COME hither, ye faithful, triumphantly sing:
   Come, se in the manger the angels' dread king!
   To Bethlehem hasten with joyful accord;
   O come ye, come hither, to worship the Lord!

2. True Son of the Father, He comes from the
                                           skies,
   To be born of a virgin He does not despise:
   To Bethlehem hasten with joyful accord;
   O come ye, come hither, to worship the Lord!

ADVENT AND CHRISTMAS.

3. Hark, hark to the angels, all singing in heaven,
"To God in the highest all glory be given!"
To Bethlehem hasten with joyful accord;
O come ye, come hither, to worship the Lord!

4. To Thee, then, o Jesus, this day of Thy birth,
Be glory and honor through heaven and earth.
True Godhead incarnate, omnipotent Word!
O come, let us hasten to worship the Lord!
E Caswall. (Adeste fideles).

III. New Year.

16

1. O LORD God Father, thanks to Thee
In this New Year we render,
For from all dangers graciously
Thou hast been our defender.
In all the year which now hath fled,
Hast giv'n us life and daily bread,
And peace to this our country.

2. Lord Jesus Christ, our thanks to Thee
In this New Year we render,
For Thou Thy people's king wilt be,

Their guardian and defender:
Thou hast redeemed them with Thy blood,
Thou art their only trust, O God,
In life and death, forever.

3. Lord Holy Ghost, our thanks to Thee
In this New Year we render,
For to Thy grace we owe that we
Enjoy Thy word's bright splendor;
Thus Thou hast given from above
Into our hearts true faith and love
And other Christian virtues.

4. O faithful Lord, our God we pray,
Grant us henceforth Thy favor,
Take graciously our sins away,
And cover them forever;
Give us a happy, blest New Year,
And when the hour of death draws near,
A blest departure. Amen.
C. Schneegas.

17

1. NOW let us raise our voices
In prayer, and let rejoice us
In God, who strength from heaven
Unto our life hath given.

2. The stream of years is flowing,
And we are onward going,
From old to new surviving,
And by His mercy thriving.

3. In woe we often languish,
And pass through times of anguish,
When fearful war aboundeth
And dread this earth surroundeth.

4. A faithful mother keepeth
Watch while her infant sleepeth,
And all its grief assuageth,
When angry tempest rageth:

5. Thus God His children shieldeth
And full protection yieldeth;
When need and woe distress them,
His loving arms caress them.

6. In vain is all our doing,
The labor we're pursuing
In our hands prospers never,
Unless God watcheth ever.

7. We praise Thy mercies gaily,
Which Thou renewest daily,
To Thee, our strong defender
From grief, our thanks we render.

8. O God of mercy, hear us;
   Our Father, be Thou near us;
   'Mid crosses and in sadness
   Be Thou our fount of gladness.

9. To all that bow before Thee
   And for Thy grace implore Thee,
   Do grant Thy benediction,
   And patience in affliction.

10. With richest blessings crown us,
    In all our ways, Lord, own us;
    Give grace, who grace bestowest,
    To all, e'en to the lowest.

11. Of all forlorn be father,
    Again the strayed sheep gather,
    And of the poor and needy
    Be Thou the succor speedy.

12. Grant help to all afflicted,
    And to all souls dejected,
    By melancholy haunted,
    May cheerful thoughts be granted.

13. All earthly gifts excelling,
    Thy Holy Ghost indwelling
    Give us, to make us glorious
    And lead to Thee victorious.

15. All this Thy hand bestoweth,
   Thou, Life, whence our life floweth;
   To me and all believers
   Grant, Lord, these New-Year's favors.
   P. Gerhardt.

18

1. GREAT God, we sing that mighty Hand,
   By which supported still we stand:
   The opening year Thy mercy shows;
   Let mercy crown it, till it close.

2. By day, by night, at home, abroad,
   Still we are guarded by our God
   By his incessant bounty fed,
   By His unerring counsel led.

3. With grateful hearts the past we own;
   The future, all to us unknown,
   We to Thy guardian care commit,
   And, peaceful, leave before Thy feet.

4. In scenes exalted or depressed,
   Be Thou our joy, and Thou our rest;
   Thy goodness all our hopes shall raise,
   Adored through all our changing days.

4. When death shall interrupt our songs,
   And seal in silence mortal tongues;
   Our Helper God, in whom we trust,
   In better worlds our souls shall boast.
   Doddridge.

IV. The Passion.

19

1. O LAMB of God, most blameless,
   Who on the cross didst languish;
   Though mocked by hatred shameless,
   E'er patient in Thine anguish:
   Thou barest our transgression,
   That we may gain salvation;
   Have mercy on us, O Jesus!

2. O Lamb of God, etc., etc.
   Have mercy on us, O Jesus!

3. O Lamb of God, etc., etc.
   Grant us Thy blessing, O Jesus!
   Decius.

20

1. OVER Cedron Jesus treadeth
   To his passion for us all;
   Every human eye be weeping.

Tears of blood for Him let fall!
Round His spirit flock the foes,
Place their shafts and bend their bows,
Aiming at the Saviour solely,
While the world forsakes Him wholly.

2. David once, with heart afflicted,
Crossed the Cedron's narrow strand,
Clouds of gloom and grief around him,
When an exile from his land.
But, O Jesus! blacker now
Rends the cloud above Thy brow,
Hasting to death's dreary portals
For the shame and sin of mortals.

3. See! how, anguish-struck, He falleth
Prostrate, and with struggling breath
Three times on His God He calleth,
Praying that the bitter death
And the cup of doom may go,
Till, replacing inward woe,
Angel-comforts round Him gather —
"Not My will, but Thine, O Father!"

4. See! how in that hour of darkness,
Battling with the evil power,
Agonies untold assail Him,

On His soul the arrows shower;
All the garden-flowers are wet
With the drops of bloody sweat,
From His anguished frame distilling—
World's redemption thus fulfilling.

5. But, O flowers, so sadly watered
By this pure and precious dew,
In some blessed hour your blossoms
'Neath the olive-shadows grew!
Paradise's gardens bear
Naught that can with you compare,
For the blood thus sprinkled o'er ye
Makes my soul the heir of glory.

6. When as flowers themselves I wither,
When I droop and fade like grass,
When the life-streams through my pulses
Dull and ever duller pass,
When at last they cease to roll,
Then to cheer my sinking soul,
Grace of Jesus, be Thou given—
Source of triumph! Pledge of heaven!

Kingo.

21

1. O BLEEDING head, and wounded,
And full of pain and scorn,
In mockery surrounded

THE PASSION.

With cruel crown of thorn!
O Head! once crowned with glory
And heavenly majesty,
But now abused and gory,
Yet here I welcome Thee!

2. O face of noble features,
Before which worlds did bow
Once dreaded by all creatures,
Men spit upon Thee now!
Whence is this deathlike whiteness?
Whose ruthless hand has quelled
Thine eyes' celestial brightness,
Which earthly lights excelled?

3. Thy cheeks' bright hue is vanished
Thy rosy lips' sweet breath
Has fled now; all has banished
The strong hand of pale Death,
Who has with cruel rigor
Bereft Thee of Thy life;
Thus Thou hast lost Thy vigor
And strength in this sad strife.

4. My burden, dearest Saviour,
Hast thus Thou borne for me,
My sinful misbehaviour

Has caused Thine agony.
Lo! I am the transgressor
Whom curse and wrath behoove:
Grant me, my intercessor,
A single glance of love!

5. My Guardian, do receive me?
My Shepherd, own me Thine!
What blessings didst Thou give me,
O Source of gifts divine!
How oft Thy mouth has fed me
With milk and sweetest food!
How oft Thy Spirit led me
To stores of heavenly good!

6. Near Thee I'll stand forever,
Oh, do not drive me back!
Lord, I will leave Thee never;
Yea, when Thy heart doth break,
And when Thy head doth languish
In death's last fatal grasp,
Then in Thy deepest anguish,
Thee in mine arms I'll clasp.

7. It fils my heart with gladness,
Gives joy unto my mind,
When in Thy pain and sadness,
My Saviour, me I find.

Ah well for me, if lying
Here at Thy feet, my Life,
I too with Thee were dying,
And thus might end my strife!

8. My heart its thanks is off'ring
To Thee, O dearest friend,
For by Thy death and suff'ring
My good Thou didst intend.
Ah! grant that I may ever
Be true to Thee in faith;
When soul and body sever,
In Thee may be my death.

9. O Lord, do Thou not leave me,
When I this world must leave,
But Thy support do give me,
When my last sigh I heave;
When soul and body languish
In death's last agony,
Then take away mine anguish
By Thine on Calvary.

10. Be Thou my consolation
And shield, when I must die,
Let me behold Thy passion,
When my last hour draws nigh;

My dim eyes then shall see Thee,
Upon Thy cross shall dwell,
My heart by faith enfold Thee;
Who dieth thus, dies well!

Bernhard of Chairvaux. P. Gerhardt.

22

1. LORD, Thy death and passion give
Strength and comfort at my need,
Every hour while here I live,
On Thy love my soul shall feed.
Doth some evil thought upstart?
Lo, Thy cross defends my heart,
Shows the peril, and I shrink
Back from loitering on the brink.

2. Doth my carnal nature yearn
After wanton joys? again
Quickly to Thy cross I turn,
And her voice is heard in vain.
Cometh strong temptation's hour,
When my foe puts forth his power?
Sheltered by this holy shield,
Soon I drive him from the field.

3. Would the world my steps entice
To yon wide and level road,
Filled with mirth, alluring vice?

Lord, I think upon the load
Thou didst once for me endure,
And I flee all thoughts impure;
Thinking on Thy bitter pains,
Hushed in prayer my heart remains.

4. Yes Thy cross hath power to heal
All the wounds of sin and strife,
Lost in Thee my heart doth feel
Sudden warmth and nobler life.
In my saddest, darkest grief
Let Thy sweetness bring relief,
Thou who camest but to save,
Thou who fearest not to grave!

5. Lord, in Thee I place my trust,
Thou art my defence and tower;
Death Thou treadest in the dust,
O'er my soul he hath no power;
That I may have part in Thee,
Help and save and comfort me,
Give me of Thy grace and might,
Resurrection, life, and light.

6. Fount of good, within me dwell,
For the peace Thy presence sheds,
Keeps us safe in conflict fell,

Charms the pain from dying beds.
Hide me safe within Thine arm,
Where no foe can hurt or harm;
Whoso, Lord, in Thee doth rest,
He hath conquered, he is blest.

J. Heermann.

23

1. ALAS! and did my Saviour bleed,
And did my Sovereign die?
Would He devote that sacred head
For such a worm as I?

2. Was it for crimes that I had done,
He groaned upon the tree?
Amazing pity! grace unknown!
And love beyond degree!

3. Well might the sun in darkness hide,
And shut his glories in,
When God the mighty Maker died
For man the creature's sin!

4. Thus might I hide my blushing face,
While His dear cross appears;
Dissolve my heart in thankfulness,
And melt my eyes in tears.

5. But drops of grief can ne'er repay
   The debt of love I owe.
   Here, Lord, I give myself away:
   'Tis all that I can do.

Watts.

24

1. WHEN I survey the wondrous cross
   On which the Prince of Glory died,
   My richest gain I count but loss,
   And poor contempt on all my pride.

2. Forbid it, Lord, that I should boast,
   Save in the death of Christ my God;
   All the vain things that charm me most,
   I sacrifice them to His blood.

3. See, from His head, His hands, His feet,
   Sorrow and love flow mingled down!
   Did e'er such love and sorrow meet,
   Or thorns compose so rich a crown?

4. Were the whole realm of nature mine,
   That were a tribute far too small;
   Love so amazing, so divine,
   Demands my soul, my life, my all.

Watts.

THE PASSION.

25

1. HAIL, Thou once despised Jesus!
   Hail, Thou Galilean King!
   Thou didst suffer to release us,
   Thou didst free salvation bring.
   Hail Thou agonizing Saviour,
   Bearer of our sin and shame!
   By Thy merits we find favor;
   Life is given through Thy name.

2. Paschal Lamb, by God appointed
   All our sins on Thee were laid;
   By almighty Love anointed,
   Thou hast full atonement made.
   All Thy people are forgiven
   Through the virtue of Thy blood;
   Opened is the gate of heaven;
   Peace is made 'twixt man and God.

3. Jesus, hail, enthroned in glory,
   There for ever to abide!
   All the heavenly hosts adore Thee,
   Seated at Thy Father's side:
   There for sinners Thou art pleading,
   There Thou dost our place prepare,
   Ever for us interceding,
   Till in glory we appear.

4. Worship, honor, power, and blessing,
   Thou art worthy to receive;
   Loudest praises, without ceasing,
   Meet it is for us to give.
   Help, ye bright, angelic spirits,
   Bring your sweetest, noblest lays,
   Help to sing our Saviour's merits,
   Help to chant Immanuel's praise.

   Bakewell.

26

1. O DARKEST Woe!
   Ye tears, forth flow!
   Has earth so sad a wonder,
   That the Father's only Son
   Now lies buried yonder!

2. O Sorrow dread!
   Our God is dead!
   But his great compassion
   By his death upon the cross
   Gained for us salvation.

3. O son of man!
   It was the ban
   Of death on thee that brought Him
   Down to suffer for thy sins,
   And such woe hath wrought Him.

4. See, stained with blood
   The Lamb of God,
   Thy bridegroom, lies before thee,
   Pouring out His life that He
   May to life restore thee.

5. O Ground of faith,
   Laid low in death!
   Sweet lips now silent sleeping!
   Surely, all that live must mourn
   Here with bitter weeping.

6. O Virgin-born,
   Thy death we mourn,
   Thou lovely Star of gladness,
   Who could see Thy reeking blood
   Void of grief and sadness?

7. Yea, blest shall be
   Forever he,
   Who ponders well this story,
   That into a tomb was laid
   He, the Lord of Glory.

8. O Jesus blest!
   My Help and Rest!

THE PASSION.

With tears, Lord, I entreat Thee:
Let me love Thee to the last,
Till in heaven I greet Thee!

Rist.

27

JESUS, O my King and Saviour,
Write Thy name within my heart,
So that world and sin may never
Blot it out with hellish art.
This inscription let it be:
Jesus Christ, on Calvary
Crucified, my adoration
E'er shall be and my salvation.

Kingo.

V. Easter.

28

1. IN Death's strong grasp the Saviour lay,
For our offences given;
But now the Lord is risen to-day
And brings us life from heaven;
Therefore let us all rejoice,
And praise our God with cheerful voice,
And sing loud Hallelujahs.

Hallelujah!

2. No son of man could conquer death,
   Such mischief sin had wrought us,
   For innocence dwelt not on earth,
   And therefore death had brought us
   Into bondage from of old,
   And ever grew more strong and bold,
   And kept us in his prison.
                             Hallelujah!

3. But Jesus Christ, God's only Son,
   Hath come to conquer for us,
   Hath put away our sins, and won
   Death's power and title o'er us.
   But the form of death is left,
   For his sting he is bereft,
   His power is lost forever.
                             Hallelujah

4. It was a strange and wondrous fray,
   When life and death contended;
   The Lord of life hath won the day,
   The reign of death is ended;
   Yea, 'tis as the Scripture saith,
   That Christ in dying conquered death,
   So that we now may scorn him.
                             Hallelujah!

5. The real Paschal Lamb is He,
   Whom God the Father gave us,
   Who died on the accursed tree,
   O wondrous love! to save us.
   See! His blood doth mark our door,
   Faith points to it, death passes o'er,
   The murderer cannot harm us.
        Hallelujah

6. Then let us keep the festival
   Whereto the Lord invites us;
   Christ is himself the joy of all,
   The Sun that warms and lights us;
   By His grace He doth impart
   Eternal sunshine to the heart;
   The night of sin is ended.
        Hallelujah!

7. Thus let us feast this Easter-day
   On Christ, the Bread of heaven:
   The word of grace hath done away
   The old and evil leaven;
   Christ Himself our souls will feed,
   He is our meat and drink indeed;
   Faith lives upon no other.
        Hallelujah!
         Luther.

29

1. AWAKE, my heart, with gladness,
   See what to-day is done!
   How after gloom and sadness
   Comes forth the glorious Sun!
   My Saviour there was laid,
   Where our bed must be made,
   When to the realms of light
   Our spirit wings its flight.

2. They in the grave did sink Him,
   The foe held jubilee;
   Before he can bethink him,
   Lo! Christ again is free,
   And Victory! He cries;
   He waveth tow'rds the skies
   His banner, for the field
   Is by the Hero held.

3. Upon the grave is standing
   The Hero, looking round;
   The foe, no more withstanding,
   His weapons on the ground
   Throws down, his hellish power
   To Christ he must give o'er,
   And to the Victor's bands
   Must yield his feet and hands

4. This is a sight that gladdens
   And fills my heart with glee;
   Now naught whatever saddens
   My soul, nor takes from me
   My happy, cheerful mood,
   Or any precious good
   Which by His victory
   Christ Jesus gained for me.

5. I fear nor hell nor devil,
   They of their power are shorn,
   I'm ever free from evil,
   And sin I laugh to scorn.
   Grim death with all its might
   Cannot my soul affright,
   It is an empty form,
   How e'er it rage and storm.

6. The world against me rageth,
   Its fury I disdain;
   The war whiche'er it wageth
   Against me, is in vain.
   No trouble troubles me,
   My heart from care is free,
   For in the darkest night
   I see the brightest light.

7. I cleave now and forever
To Christ, a member true,
My Head will leave me never,
Whate'er He passeth through;
He treads the world beneath
His feet, and conquers death
And hell, and breaks sin's thrall;
I follow him through all.

8. To glory He ascendeth,
I follow Him fore'er,
For He, my Head, defendeth
His member from all care;
No enemy I fear,
While He, my Head, is near;
My Saviour is my shield,
By Him all rage is stilled.

9. He to the gates me leadeth
Of yon fair realms of light,
Whereon the pilgrim readeth
In golden letters bright:
"Who there are scorned with me,
With me here crowned shall be;
Who there with me shall die,
Shall here be raised as I!"

P. Gerhardt.

30

1. JESUS Christ, my sure Defence
   And my Saviour, ever liveth;
   Knowing this, my confidence
   Rests upon the hope it giveth,
   Though the night of death be fraught
   Still with many an anxious thought.

2. Jesus, my Redeemer, lives!
   I, too, unto life must waken;
   Endless joys my Saviour gives;
   Shall my courage then be shaken?
   Shall I fear? Or could the Head
   Rise and leave His members dead?

3. Nay, too closely am I bound
   Unto Him by hope for ever;
   Faith's strong hand the Rock hath **found**,
   Grasped it, and will leave it never;
   Not the ban of death can part
   From its Lord the trusting heart.

4. I am only flesh and blood,
   And on this corruption seizeth,
   But I know, my Lord and God
   From the grave my body raiseth,
   That with him eternally
   In His glory I may be.

5. Glorified I shall again
   Be with this my skin enshrouded,
   In my body I shall then
   See the Lord with eyes unclouded,
   I in this my flesh shall see
   Jesus Christ eternally.

6. I shall see Him with these eyes,
   And shall know my Lord and Saviour,
   Not another shall I rise,
   I shall see and love Him ever;
   Only there shall disappear
   Weakness in and round me here.

7. What here sickens, mourns, and sighs,
   Christ with Him in glory bringeth;
   Earthly is the seed, and dies,
   Heavenly from the grave it springeth;
   Natural is the death we die,
   Spiritual, our life on High.

8. Then take comfort, nay, rejoice,
   For His members Christ will cherish;
   Fear not, they will know His voice,
   Though awhile they seem to perish,
   When the final trump is heard,
   And the deaf, cold grave is stirred.

9. Laugh to scorn the gloomy grave,
   And at death no longer tremble,
   For the Lord who comes to save,
   Round Him shall His saints assemble,
   Raising them o'er all their foes,
   Mortal weakness, fear, and woes.

10. Only draw away your heart
    Now from pleasures base and hollow;
    Would ye there with Christ have part,
    Here His footsteps ye must follow;
    Fix your heart beyond the skies,
    Whither ye yourselves would rise!
    Louisa Henrietta of Brandenburg.

31

1. CHRIST the Lord is risen to-day,
   Sons of men and angels say.
   Raise your joys and triumph high;
   Sing, ye heavens, and earth reply.

2. Love's redeeming work is done,
   Fought the fight, the battle won;
   Lo! the Sun's eclipse is o'er;
   Lo! He sets in blood no more.

3. Vain the stone, the watch, the seal;
   Christ has burst the gates of hell!
   Death in vain forbids His rise;
   Christ has opened paradise.

4. Lives again our glorious King;
   Where, O death, is now thy sting?
   Dying once, He all doth save;
   Where thy victory, O grave?

5. Soar we now where Christ has led
   Following our exalted Head;
   Made like Him, like Him we rise;
   Ours the cross, the grave, the skies!

6. Hail the Lord of earth and heaven!
   Praise to Thee by both be given:
   Thee we greet triumphant now;
   Hail, the Resurrection Thou!
   C. Wesley.

32

1. WHO is this that comes from Edom,
   All His raiment stained with blood,
   To the captive speaking freedom,
   Bringing and bestowing good;
   Glorious in the garb He wears,
   Glorious in the spoil He bears?

EASTER.

2. 'Tis the Saviour, now victorious,
Travelling onward in His might;
'Tis the Saviour; O how glorious
To His people is the sight!
Satan conquered and the grave!
Jesus now is strong to save.

3. Why that blood His raiment staining?
'Tis the blood of many slain;
Of His foes there's none remaining,
None the contest to maintain.
Fallen they are, no more to rise;
All their glory prostrate lies.

4. Mighty Victor! reign forever,
Wear the crown so dearly won;
Never shall Thy people, never,
Cease to sing what Thou hast done:
Thou hast fought Thy people's foes,
Thou hast healed Thy people's woes.

Th. Kelly.

33

1. I KNOW that my Redeemer lives.
What comfort this sweet sentence gives!
He lives, He lives, who once was dead,
He lives, my ever-living Head.

2. He lives to bless me with His love,
   He lives to plead for me above,
   He lives my hungry soul to feed,
   He lives to help in time of need.

3. He lives to grant me rich supply,
   He lives to guide me with His eye,
   He lives to comfort me when faint,
   He lives to hear my soul's complaint.

4. He lives to silence all my fears,
   He lives to wipe away my tears,
   He lives to calm my troubled heart.
   He lives all blessings to impart.

5. He lives, and grants me daily breath,
   He lives, and I shall conquer death;
   He lives my mansion to prepare,
   He lives to bring me safely there.

6. He lives, all glory to His name!
   He lives, my Jesus, still the same;
   O heavenly joy this sentence gives:
   I know that my Redeemer lives!

   S. Medley.

34

1. JESUS lives, He bursts the grave,
   In His Godhead's power He riseth:
   Now the surest proof we have
   That His blood and death sufficeth.
   Lightnings flash, earth quaking cleaveth,
   Graves are opened — Jesus liveth.

2. I'm victorious since for me,
   Jesus bound the foe to mortals,
   Swallowed death in victory,
   Opened wide the heavenly portals,
   Gave to me a freedom glorious —
   In the Lord I am victorious.

I. N. Brun.

VI. Ascension.

35

1. SINCE Christ has gone to heaven, His home,
   I too that home one day shall share,
   And in this hope I overcome
   All doubt, all anguish, and despair;
   For where the Head is, well we know,
   The members He hath left below
   In time He surely gathers there.

2. Since Christ has reached His glorious throne
   And mighty gifts henceforth are His,
   My heart can rest in heaven alone,
   On earth my Lord I ever miss;
   I long to be with Him on high,
   My heart and thoughts do always fly,
   Where now my only treasure is.

3. From Thy ascension let such grace,
   Dear Lord, be ever found in me,
   That steadfast faith may guide my ways
   With step unfaltering up to Thee,
   And at Thy voice I may depart
   With joy to dwell where Thou, Lord, art.
   O Saviour, grant this prayer to me!

   Wegelin.

36

1. DRAW us to Thee, Lord Jesus,
   And we will hasten on;
   For strong desire doth seize us
   To go where Thou art gone.

2. Draw us to Thee; enlighten
   Our hearts to find Thy way,
   That else the tempests frighten,
   Or pleasures lure astray.

ASCENSION.

3. Draw us to Thee, and teach us
E'en now that rest to find,
Where turmoils cannot reach us,
Nor cares weigh down our mind.

4. Draw us to Thee; nor leave us
Till all our path is trod,
Then in Thine arms receive us,
And bear us home to God.
Lud. Elisabeth,
Countess of Schwarzburg-Rudolstadt.

37

1. OUR Lord is risen from the dead;
Our Jesus is gone up on high:
The powers of hell are captive led,
Dragged to the portals of the sky.

2. There His triumphal chariot waits,
And angels chant the solemn lay:
Lift up your heads, ye heavenly gates!
Ye everlasting doors, give way!

3. Loose all your bars of massy light,
And wide unfold the radiant scene:
He claims these mansions as His right;
Receive the King of Glory in.

ASCENSION.

4. Who is the King of Glory? Who?
   The Lord, that all His foes o'ercame,
   The world, sin, death, and hell o'erthrew;
   And Jesus is the Conqueror's name.
                                    C. Wesley.

VII. Whitsuntide.

38

1. COME, Holy Spirit, God and Lord!
   Be all Thy graces now outpoured
   On Thy believers' soul and heart,
   Thy fervent love to them impart.
   Lord, by the brightness of Thy light
   Thou in the faith dost men unite
   Of every tongue and every nation;
   We therefore sing with exultation:
                   Hallelujah! Hallelujah!

2. Thou Holy Light and Guide divine,
   Oh cause the word of life to shine,
   Teach us to know our God aright
   And call Him Father with delight.
   From doctrines strange our souls defend,
   That they on Christ alone attend,

In Him with living faith abiding,
In Him with all their might confiding.
    Hallelujah! Hallelujah!

3. Thou Holy Fire, sweet Source of rest,
Grant that, with joy and hope possessed,
We in thy service ever stay,
And trouble drive us not away.
Lord, let Thy power prepare our heart,
To our weak nature strength impart,
That firmly here we be contending,
Through death and life to Thee ascending.
    Hallelujah! Hallelujah!
M. Luther.

39

1. WE pray Thee, Lord God Holy Ghost,
Grant, what of all things we need the most,
Living faith, so that when life is ending
From this vale of tears we home be wending.
    Kyrie eleison!

2. Shine in our hearts, Thou worthy Light,
Teach us Jesus Christ to know aright,
That we cling to Him, our faithful Saviour,
Who has gained us heavenly bliss forever!
    Kyrie eleison!

3. O heavenly Love, grant us Thy grace,
Fervent love let in our hearts have place,
So that truly we may love each other,
Live in constant peace with every brother.
      Kyrie eleison!

4. Best Comforter in every need,
Grant that neither shame nor death we heed,
That our heart its courage never loseth,
When the old arch-fiend our life accuseth.
      Kyrie eleison!
       M. Luther.

40

1. O HOLY Spirit, enter in,
Among these hearts Thy work begin,
Thy temple deign to make us;
Sun of the soul, Thou Light divine,
Around and in us brightly shine,
To strength and gladness wake us,
That we To Thee
Truly living, To Thee giving
Prayer unceasing,
Still may be in love increasing.

2. Impressive power, O Lord, impart
E'er to Thy word, that in our heart
As fire it may be blazing,

That God the Father, and the Son,
And Spirit, Holy Three in One,
True God we e'er be praising.
Lord, stay, And sway
Our souls ever, That they never
May forsake Thee,
But by faith their refuge make Thee.

3. Thou Fountain, whence all wisdom flows
Which God on pious hearts bestows,
Grant us Thy consolation,
That in our pure faith's unity
We bear true witness, Lord, of Thee
For all the world's salvation.
Hear us, Cheer us
By Thy teaching, Let our preaching
And our labors
Praise Thee, Lord, and aid our neighbors.

4. Left to ourselves we can but stray:
O lead us in the narrow way,
With wisest counsels guide us;
And give us steadfastness, that we
May ever faithful prove to Thee,
Whatever woes betide us.
Lord, now Heal Thou
All hearts broken, Give some token

Thou art near us,
Whom we trust to light and cheer us.

5. Thy balm of strength, Lord, let us feel,
That Christian chivalry and zeal
Thus in us may be thriving,
That under Thy protection we
All adversaries may defy,
While we on earth are living.
Descend, Defend
From all errors And earth's terrors;
Thy protection
Grant us, Lord, in our affliction.

6. Thou mighty Rock and Source of life,
Let Thy dear word, 'mid doubt and strife
So in our hearts be burning,
That we be faithful unto death
In Thy pure love and holy faith,
From Thee true wisdom learning.
Thy grace, Thy peace
On us shower; By Thy power
Christ confessing,
Let us win our Saviour's blessing.

7. O gentle Dew, from heaven now fall
With power upon the hearts of all,

Thy tender love instilling;
That heart to heart more closely bound
In kindly deeds be fruitful found,
The law of love fulfilling.
O Life, No strife
Then shall grieve Thee, We receive Thee,
  Where Thou livest,
Peace and love and joy Thou givest.

8. Grant that our days, while life shall last,
In truth and holiness be passed,
Be Thou our strength forever,
So that we henceforth may be free
From carnal lusts and vanity,
Which us from Thee would sever.
Keep Thou Pure now
From offences Heart and senses,
Holy Spirit,
That God's kingdom we inherit.

Schirmer.

41

1. COME, Holy Spirit, heavenly Dove,
With all Thy quickening powers;
Kindle a flame of sacred love
In these cold hearts of ours.

2. See how we grovel here below,
   Fond of these earthly toys;
   Our souls, how heavily they go
   To reach eternal joys.

3. Dear Lord, and shall we always live
   At this poor, dying rate?
   Our love so cold, so faint to Thee,
   And Thine to us so great?

4. Come, Holy Spirit, heavenly Dove,
   With all Thy quickening powers;
   Come, shed abroad a Saviour's love,
   And that shall kindle ours.

   Watts.

VIII. Trinity.

42

1. THOU who art Three in Unity,
   True God from all eternity;
   The sun is fading from our sight:
   Let on us shine Thy heavenly light.

2. We praise Thee, Lord, at break of day,
   At night we also to Thee pray;
   With our poor song we worship Thee
   Now, ever, and eternally.

3. E'er God the Father be adored,
And God the Son, the only Lord,
And God the Holy Spirit we
Will praise to all eternity.

Ambrose. Luther.

43

1. PRAISED be the Lord, my God,
My Light, my Life from heaven,
My Maker, who to me
Hath soul and body given,
My Father, who protects
My life from infancy,
Who always hath bestowed
Great gifts of love on me.

2. Praised be the Lord, my God,
My Bliss, my Life from heaven,
The Father's loved Son,
Who for mankind was given,
Who hath atoned for me
With His most precious blood,
Who giveth to my faith
The greatest heavenly good.

3. Praised be the Lord, my God,
My Trust, my Life from heaven,

The Father's Spirit, whom
The Son to me hath given,
He who revives my heart
And gives new strength and power,
Aid, comfort, and support
In sorrow's gloomy hour.

4. Praised be the Lord, my God,
He who forever liveth,
To whom the heavenly host
E'er praise and honor giveth;
Praised be the Lord, our God,
In whose great name we boast,
The Father, God the Son,
And God the Holy Ghost;

5. To whom our praise we give,
With joy our offerings bringing,
And with the angels' hosts
The "Holy! Holy!" singing;
He whom all Christendom
Doth praise most joyfully,
Praised be the Lord, my God,
To all eternity!

Olearius.

44

1. FATHER of all! whose love profound
A ransom for our souls hath found,
Before Thy throne we sinners bend:
To us Thy pardoning love extend.

2. Almighty Son! Incarnate Word!
Our Prophet, Priest, Redeemer, Lord!
Before Thy throne we sinners bend:
To us Thy saving grace extend.

3. Eternal Spirit! by whose breath
The soul is raised from sin and death,
Before Thy throne we sinners bend:
To us Thy quickening power extend.

4. Jehovah! Father, Spirit, Son,
Mysterious Godhead! Three in One!
Before Thy throne we sinners bend:
Grace, pardon, life, to us extend.

John Couper.

IX. Reformation.

45

1. A MIGHTY fortress is our God,
   A trusty shield and weapon;
   He helps us free from every need
   That hath us now o'ertaken.
   The old bitter foe
   Means us deadly woe:
   Deep guile and great might
   Are his dread arms in fight,
   On earth is not his equal.

2. With might of ours can naught be done,
   Soon were our loss effected;
   But for us fights the Valiant One
   Whom God himself elected.
   Ask ye, Who is this? —
   Jesus Christ it is,
   Lord of Sabaoth,
   There is no other God,
   He holds the field for ever.

3. Though devils all the world should fill,
   All watching to devour us,
   We tremble not, we fear no ill,
   They cannot overpower us.

This world's prince may still
Scowl fierce as he will,
He can harm us none,
He's judged, the deed is done,
One little word o'erthrows him.

4. The word they still shall let remain,
Nor any thank have for it,
The Lord's with us upon the plain
With His good gifts and Spirit;
Take they then our life,
Goods, fame, child and wife,
When their worst is done,
They yet have nothing won:
The Kingdom ours remaineth.

Luther.

46

1. LORD, keep us steadfast in Thy word,
And break the Pope's and Turk's fell sword,
Who fain would hurl from off Thy throne
Christ Jesus, Thy beloved Son.

2. Lord Jesus Christ, Thy power make known
For Thou art Lord of Lords alone;
Defend Thy Christendom, that we
May evermore sing praise to Thee.

3. O Holy Ghost, best comfort Thou,
   With unity Thy church endow,
   Support us in our final strife,
   And lead us out of death to life.

4. Destroy their counsels, Lord our God,
   And smite them with an iron rod,
   And let them fall into the snare
   Which for Thy Christians they prepare;

5. So that at last they may perceive
   That, Lord our God, Thou still dost live,
   And dost deliver mightily
   All those who put their trust in Thee.
   Luther. V. 4 & 5 by Jonas.

47

1. FEAR not, O little flock, the foe
   Who madly seeks your overthrow;
   Dread not his rage and power:
   What though your courage sometimes faints,
   His seeming triumph o'er God's saints
   Lasts but a little hour.

2. Be of good cheer; your cause belongs
   To Him who can avenge your wrongs;
   Leave it to Him, our Lord.

Though hidden yet from mortal eyes
His Gideon shall for you arise,
Uphold you and His word.

3. As true as God's own word is true,
Not earth nor hell with all their crew
Against us shall prevail.
A jest and byword are they grown;
God is with us; we are His own:
Our victory cannot fail.
Gustavus Adolphus.

X. The Word of God and the Church.

48

1. LORD Jesus Christ, with us abide,
For round us falls the evening tide;
Nor let Thy word, that shining light,
For us be ever veiled in night.

2. Lord, in the last sad times we live,
Therefore true steadfastness do give,
That we Thy word and sacrament
May pure retain, till life is spent.

3. Lord Jesus, help! Thy Church uphold,
   For we are sluggish, thoughtless, cold;
   Indue Thy word with power and grace,
   And spread its truth in every place.

4. O keep us in thy word, we pray;
   The guile and rage of Satan stay.
   Unto Thy Church give concord, peace,
   Zeal, courage, patience, love, and grace.

5. O God! how sin's dread works abound;
   Throughout the earth no rest is found,
   And wide has falsehood's spirit spread,
   And error boldly rears its head.

6. Those vain, presumptuous minds restrain,
   That fain would o'er Thy Christians reign,
   And e'er bring forth some fancies new,
   Devised to change Thy doctrine true.

7. The cause and glory, dearest Lord,
   Are Thine, not ours — do Thou afford
   Us help and strength and constancy;
   We ever put our trust in Thee.

8. Thy word is e'er our two-edged sword,
   Thy people's sure defense; O Lord,

Grant that in us it may abide,
So that we seek no other guide.

9. O grant that in Thy holy word
We here may live and die, good Lord,
That, when our journey endeth here,
We enter into glory there.

Selnecker.

49

1. CHRIST, Thou the champion of the band who own
Thy cross, O make Thy succor quickly known;
The schemes of those who long our blood have sought
Bring Thou to nought.

2. Do Thou Thyself for us Thy children fight,
Withstand the devil, quell his rage and might;
Whate'er assails Thy members left below,
Do Thou o'erthrow.

3. Peace, O Lord, grant us; peace in church and school,
Peace to the powers who o'er our country rule,
Peace to the conscience, peace within the heart,
Do Thou impart.

4. So shall Thy goodness here be still adored,
   Thou Guardian of Thy little flock, dear Lord.
   Yea, heaven and earth through all eternity
   Shall worship Thee.
   Loewenstern.

50

1. LET me be Thine forever,
   Thou faithful God and Lord,
   May I forsake Thee never,
   Nor wander from Thy word;
   Keep me from error's mazes,
   Lord, give me constancy,
   And I will sing Thy praises
   Through all eternity.

2. Lord Jesus, my salvation,
   My Love and Life divine,
   My only Consolation,
   To Thee I all resign;
   For Thou hast dearly bought me
   With blood and bitter pain,
   Let me, since Thou hast sought me,
   Eternal life obtain.

3. And Thou, O Holy Spirit,
   My Comforter and Guide,
   In my Redeemer's merit
   Let ever me confide,

His holy name confessing.
Help me when death draws nigh;
Grant me Thy constant blessing,
And save me when I die.

Selnecker.

51

1. O CHRIST, our true and only Light,
Enlighten those who dwell in night;
Let those afar now hear Thy voice,
And in Thy fold with us rejoice.

2. Fill with the radiance of Thy grace
The souls now lost in error's maze,
And all whom in their secret minds
Some dark delusion hurts and blinds.

3. And all who else have strayed from Thee,
O gently seek! Thy healing be
To every wounded conscience given,
And let them also share Thy heaven.

4. O make the deaf to hear Thy word,
And teach the dumb to speak, dear Lord,
Who dare not yet Thy faith avow,
Though secretly they hold it now.

5. Shine on the darkened and the cold,
Recall the wanderers to Thy fold,
Unite all those who walk apart,
Confirm the weak and doubting heart.

6. So shall they with us evermore
Thy grace with wondering thanks adore,
And praise unceasing Thee be given
By all Thy Church in earth and heaven.
J. Heermann.

52

1. FROM Greenland's icy mountains,
From India's coral strand;
Where Afric's sunny fountains
Roll down their golden sand;
From many an ancient river,
From many a palmy plain,
They call us to deliver
Their land from error's chain.

2. What though the spicy breezes
Blow soft o'er Ceylon's isle;
Though every prospect pleases,
And only man is vile:
In vain with lavish kindness
The gifts of God are strown:

The heathen in his blindness
Bows down to wood and stone.

3. Shall we, whose souls are lighted
With wisdom from on high,
Shall we to men benighted
The lamp of life deny?
Salvation, O salvation!
The joyful sound proclaim,
Till each remotest nation
Has learned Messiah's name.

4. Waft, waft, ye winds, His story,
And you, ye waters, roll,
Till, like a sea of glory,
It spreads from pole to pole;
Till o'er our ransomed nature
The Lamb, for sinners slain,
Reedemer, King, Creator,
In bliss returns to reign.

Heber.

XI. The Catechism.

53

1. LORD GOD, to us fore'er secure
'The catechism's instruction pure,

By Luther, servant Thine, set forth
To plant in youth Thy saving word.

2. That we may learn Thy holy will,
Bewail our sins and faults, and still
Believe in Thee and in Thy son,
Enlightened by Thy Spirit's boon.

3. That we to Thee, our Father, call
Who canst and wilt bring help to all,
That, children Thine in Baptism made,
We always Christian lives may lead.

4. That if we fall, we rise again,
And in true faith confess our sin,
And comfort by Thy Supper gain.
Grant us a happy end. Amen.

Helmbold.

54.

1. O MY CHILD, fear God the Lord,
Do not take in vain His word,
Holy keep the Sabbath day,
To thy parents honor pay,
Kill not, shun adultery,
Steal not, lies and slander flee,
Keep from covetousness free

2. In the Father I believe,
   Who to all their being gave,
   And in His incarnate Son,
   Who for man salvation won,
   Also in the Holy Ghost,
   In whose hallowing grace I trust,
   who will raise me from the dust.

3. Father dear, who art in heaven,
   To Thy name e'er praise be given,
   Unto us Thy kingdom come,
   Everywhere Thy will be done,
   Give us bread, our sins forgive,
   Let no tempter us deceive,
   From all evil us relieve.

4. Father, Son and Holy Ghost,
   Triune God, in Thee I boast,
   Thou with water and the word
   Didst baptize me, gracious Lord;
   Grant that I may faithful be,
   That I ever trust in Thee,
   And be Thine eternally.

5. Dearest Lord, my soul do feed
   With Thy flesh and real bread,
   And refresh me, Saviour mine,

With Thy blood and real wine,
In remembrance, Lord, of Thee;
Grant forgiveness thus to me.
Unto Thee be praise for aye!

B Pedersen.

55.

1. THAT MEN a godly life might live,
God did these ten Commandments give
By His true servant Moses, high
Upon the mount of Sinai.
Kyrie eleison.

2. I am thy Lord and God alone,
No other god beside me own:
Put thy whole confidence in me,
And love me in sincerity.
Kyrie eleison.

3. By idle word and speech profane
Take not my holy name in vain;
And praise not aught as good and true,
Save what thy God doth say and do.
Kyrie eleison

4. The day keep holy which God blessed,
That thou and all thy house may rest;
Keep hand and heart from labor free,
That God may have His work in thee.
Kyrie eleison.

5. Give to thy parents honor due,
   Obedient be, and loving too,
   And help them when their strength decays;
   So shall God give thee length of days.
   Kyrie eleison.

6. Harbor no hatred nor ill will,
   Lest hate breed anger, and thou kill;
   Be patient and of gentle mood,
   And to thine enemy do good.
   Kyrie eleison.

7. Be faithful to thy marriage vows,
   Thy heart give only to thy spouse;
   Keep pure thy life, and, lest thou sin,
   Use temperance and discipline.
   Kyrie eleison.

8. Steal not; all usury abhor,
   Nor wring the life-blood from the poor;
   But open wide thy loving hand,
   To aid the needy in the land.
   Kyrie eleison.

9. Bear not false witness, nor belie
   Thy neighbor by foul calumny:
   Defend his innocence from blame,
   And hide with charity his shame.
   Kyrie eleison.

10.. Thy neighbor's house desire thou not,
His wife, nor aught that he has got;
But wish that his such good may be,
As thine own heart desires for thee.
Kyrie eleison.

11. God these commandments gave, therein
To show thee, child of man, thy sin,
And make thee also well perceive
How unto God man ought to live.
Kyrie eleison.

12. Help us, Lord Jesus Christ, for we
Our Mediator have in The;
Our works can ne'er salvation gain,
They merit only endless pain.
Kyrie eleison.
Luther.

56

1. WE ALL believe in one true God,
Maker of the earth and heaven,
The Father, who to us in love
Hath the right of children given.
He both soul and body feedeth,
All we want His hand provides us;
Through the snares and perils leadeth,

Watches that no harm betide us;
He cares for us by day and night,
All things are governed by His might.

2. And we believe in God's own Son,
Jesus Christ, our Lord, possessing
An equal Godhead, might, and throne,
Source of every joy and blessing;
Conceived of the Holy Spirit,
Born of Mary, virgin mother;
That lost man might life inherit
Made true man, our elder brother
Was crucified for sinful men,
By God raised up to life again.

3. And we confess the Holy Ghost,
Who sweet grace and comfort giveth,
And with the Father and the Son
In eternal glory liveth;
Who all Christendom doth even
Keep in unity and spirit;
Sins are truly here forgiven
Through the blessed Redeemer's merit;
Our flesh will rise again, and we
Shall live with God eternally. Amen.

Luther.

57

1. OUR FATHER dear in heaven above,
Who biddest us to dwell in love,
As brethren of one family,
And pray for all we need to Thee;
Teach us to mean the words we say,
And from our inmost heart to pray.

2. Thy name be hallowed! help us, Lord,
To keep in purity Thy word,
And lead, according to Thy name,
A holy life, untouched by blame;
Let no false doctrines do us hurt,
All poor deluded souls convert.

3. Thy kingdom come! Thine let it be
In time, and through eternity!
O let Thy Holy Spirit dwell
With us, to rule and guide us well;
Break Satan's power, his rage restrain,
Despite his craft Thy church maintain.

4. Thy will be done, Lord God, in love
On earth, as 't is in heaven above!
Patience in time of grief bestow,
Obedience true in weal and woe,
Curb flesh and blood, and every ill
That sets itself against Thy will.

5. Give us this day our daily bread
And all that for this life we need!
From war and strife be our defence,
From famine and from pestilence,
That we may live in godly peace,
Free from all care and avarice.

6. Lord, all our trespasses forgive,
That they our hearts no more may grieve,
As we forgive their trespasses
Who unto us have done amiss;
Let us delight in serving Thee
In perfect love and unity.

7. Into temptation lead us not!
And when the foe doth war and plot
Against our souls on every hand,
Then, armed with faith, O may we stand
Against him as a valiant host,
Through comfort of the Holy Ghost.

8. Deliver us from evil, Lord!
In these sad times Thy help afford;
O save us from eternal death,
Console us when we yield our breath;
Grant us a blessed end, and take
Our souls to Thee for Jesus' sake.

9. Amen! that is, so let it be!
   Increase our faith continually,
   That doubting not we may believe
   That what we ask we shall receive;
   Thus at Thy name and at Thy word
   We say Amen; O hear us, Lord!
   Luther.

58

1. BLESSED Jesus, here we stand,
   Met to do as Thou hast spoken,
   And this child, at Thy command,
   Now we bring to Thee, in token
   That to Thee it here is given;
   For of such shall be Thy heaven.

2. Yea, Thy warning voice is plain,
   And with solemn awe we hear it:
   "He who is not born again
   Of the water and the Spirit
   In Thy fold no place is given,
   Can not enter realm of heaven."

3. Therefore hasten we to Thee,
   Take the pledge we bring, O take it,
   Show Thy glorious mercy free,
   And in tender pity make it

Now Thy child, and leave it never,
Thine on earth, and Thine forever.

4. Wash it, Jesus, in Thy blood
From its nature's inborn tarnish;
Let it, risen from this flood,
Have Thy purple robe its garnish;
Cover all its sins forever
By Thine innocence, O Saviour.

5. Turn the darkness into light,
Change Thy wrath to gracious favor;
Heal the serpent's cruel bite
By this wonder-working laver
Here let flow the Jordan river,
From sin's leprosy deliver.

6. Head, make it Thy member now;
Shepherd, take Thy lamb, and feed it;
Prince of peace, its peace be Thou;
Way of life, to heaven lead it;
Vine, this branch let nothing sever,
Be it graft in Thee forever!

7. Now upon Thy heart it lies,
What our hearts so dearly treasure;
Heavenward lead our burdened sighs,
Pour Thy blessing without measure;

Write the name we now have given,
Write it in the book of heaven.

B. Schmolk.

59

1. BAPTIZED into Thy name most holy,
   O Father, Son, and Holy Ghost,
   I claim a place, though weak and lowly,
   Among Thy seed, Thy chosen host;
   Buried with Christ, and dead to sin,
   Thy Spirit now shall live within.

2. My loving Father, Thou didst take me
   To be Thy child and very heir;
   My faithful Saviour, Thou didst make me
   The fruit of all Thy sorrows share;
   Thou, Spirit, wilt my comfort be
   When sore distress encompass me.

3. And I have vowed to fear and love Thee,
   And to obey Thee, Lord, alone;
   I felt Thy Holy Spirit move me,
   And freely pledged myself Thine own,
   Renouncing sin, to keep the faith,
   And war with evil unto death.

4. My faithful God, Thou failest never,
   Thy covenant surely will abide;

O cast me not away forever,
If I should stray from Thee, my Guide;
But if I fall, hide not Thy face,
Restore Thy child, Lord, by Thy grace.

5. Yea, all I am and love most dearly,
To Thee I offer now the whole;
O let me make my vows sincerely,
Take full possession of my soul!
Let naught within me, naught I own,
Serve any will save Thine alone.

6. Hence, Prince of darkness, hence forever,
For I belong now to my God!
'Tis true, I sinned; but my dear Saviour
Hath cleansed me with His holy blood.
Away, vain world, sin, leave me now,
I turn from you; God hears my vow.

7. And never let my purpose falter,
O Father, Son, and Holy Ghost,
But keep me faithful to Thine altar,
Until I join the heavenly host;
So unto Thee I live and die,
And praise Thee evermore on high.

J. J. Rambach.

60

1. JESUS Christ, our blessed Saviour,
   Turned away God's wrath forever;
   Suffering pains no tongue can tell
   He saved us from the pains of hell.

2. In remembrance of His bloody
   Death, He bade us eat His body,
   Hidden in the bread, its shrine,
   And drink His blood in sacred wine.

3. Whoso to this board repaireth,
   Take good heed how he prepareth;
   Death instead of life will he
   Receive who comes unworthily.

4. Praise the Father dear in heaven,
   Who such heavenly food hath given,
   And for sins which thou hast done
   Hath caused to die His own dear Son.

5. Thy belief let not be shaken
   That this food is to be taken
   By the sick who grieve at sin,
   Whose heavy heart is sore within.

6. To such grace and mercy turneth
   Every soul that truly mourneth;

Art thou well? avoid this board,
Lest thou receive an ill reward.

7. Christ says: Come, ye heavy laden,
I your weary hearts will gladden,
A physician do not need
Those that are whole and strong and glad.

8. Could'st thou earn thine own salvation,
Useless were my death and passion;
Wilt thou thine own helper be?
This table is not spread for thee.

9. If thou this believest truly,
And confession makest duly,
Thou a welcome guest art here,
This heavenly food thy soul will cheer.

10. For thy Saviour's glory labor;
Thou shalt truly love thy neighbor,
Such true love let him receive,
As unto thee Thy God doth give.
Huss. — Luther.

61

1. DECK thyself, my soul, with gladness,
Leave the gloomy haunts of sadness,
Come into the day-light's splendor,
There with joy thy praises render

Unto Him whose grace unbounded
Hath this wondrous banquet founded;
High o'er all the heavens He reigneth,
Yet to dwell with thee He deigneth.

2. Hasten as a bride to meet Him,
And with loving reverence greet Him,
For with words of life immortal
Now He knocketh at thy portal;
Haste to ope the gates before Him,
Saying, while thou dost adore Him:
"Suffer, Lord, that I receive Thee,
And I never more will leave Thee."

3. He who precious goods desireth
To obtain, much gold requireth;
But to give us every treasure
Of Thy love, is Thy good pleasure;
For there is on earth no coffer
Which as payment we might offer
For this cup, Thy blood containing,
And this manna, on us raining.

4. Ah, how hungers all my spirit
For the love I do not merit!
Oft have I, with sighs fast thronging,
Thought upon this food with longing,

In the battle well-nigh worsted,
For this cup of life I thirsted,
For the Friend who here invites us,
And to God Himself unites us.

5. Now I sink before Thee lowly,
Filled with joy most deep and holy,
As with trembling awe and wonder
On Thy mighty works I ponder:
How, by mystery surrounded,
Depths no man hath ever sounded
None may dare to pierce unbidden,
Secrets that with Thee are hidden.

6. Human wisdom vainly ponders,
It will ne'er explain these wonders,
That this bread doth never perish,
Although millions it doth nourish;
And that Christ His blood is giving
With the wine we are receiving.
Ah! these mysteries unsounded
Are by God alone expounded.

7. Sun who all my life dost brighten,
Light, who dost my soul enlighten,
Joy, the sweetest, man e'er knoweth,
Fount, whence all my being floweth,

At Thy feet I cry, my Maker,
Let me be a fit partaker,
Of this blessed food from heaven,
For our good, Thy glory, given.

8. Lord, Thy holy love hath driven
Thee to leave Thy throne in heaven,
For us on the cross to languish,
And to die in bitter anguish,
To forego all joy and gladness,
And to shed Thy blood in sadness.
Now we drink this blood, and never
Will forget Thy love, dear Saviour.

9. Christ, true bread of Life, I pray Thee,
Let me gladly here obey Thee,
Never to my hurt invited,
Be Thy love with love requited;
From this banquet let me measure,
Lord, how vast and deep its treasure;
Through the gifts Thou here dost give me.
As Thy guest in heaven receive me.

John Franck.

62

1. O JESUS, dearest Lord, to Thee
My fervent thanks shall ever be,
Which now Thy love on me bestowed.
For Thy true flesh and precious blood

2. Break forth in praise, rejoice, my heart:
Exceeding riches is my part,
My Jesus now in me doth dwell;
My joy and bliss no tongue can tell.
Kingo.

XII. Repentance.

63

1. OUT of the depths I cry to Thee,
Lord, hear me, I implore Thee!
Bend down Thy gracious ear to me,
My prayer let come before Thee!
If Thou remember each misdeed,
If each should have its rightful meed,
Who may abide Thy presence?

2. Our pardon is Thy gift, Thy love
And grace alone avail us;
Our works could ne'er our guilt **remove,**
The strictest life must fail us,
Before Thee none of aught can boast,
We're 'midst our fairest actions lost,
And live alone through mercy.

3. Therefore my hope is in His grace,
   And not in my own merit;
   On Him my confidence I place,
   Instructed by His Spirit;
   His precious word hath promised me
   He will my joy and comfort be,
   Thereon is my reliance.

4. And though it tarry till the night,
   And round till morning waken,
   My heart shall ne'er mistrust His might,
   Nor count itself forsaken.
   Do thus, O ye of Israel's seed,
   Ye of the Spirit born indeed,
   Wait for your God's appearing.

5. Though great our sins and sore our woes,
   His grace much more aboundeth;
   His helping love no limit knows,
   Our utmost need it soundeth.
   Our Shepherd kind and true is He,
   Who shall at last set Israel free
   From all their sin and sorrow.

Luther.

REPENTANCE.

64

1. LORD Jesus Christ, in Thee alone
My only hope on earth I place;
For other comforter is none,
No help have I but in Thy grace.
There is no man nor creature here,
No angel in the heavenly sphere,
Who at my need can succor me;
    I cry to Thee,
For Thou canst end my misery.

2. My sin is very sore and great,
I mourn beneath its horrid load;
O free me from this heavy weight,
My saviour, through Thy precious blood;-
And with Thy Father for me plead
That Thou hast suffered in my stead;
From me the burden then is rolled;
    Lord, I lay hold
On Thy dear promises of old.

3. And of Thy mercy now bestow
True Christian faith on me, O Lord!
That all the sweetness I may know
Which in Thy holy cross is stored,
Love Thee o'er earthly pride or pelf,
And love my neighbor as myself;

And when at last is come my end,
   Be Thou my friend,
From all assaults my soul defend.

4. Glory to God in highest heaven,
   The Father of eternal love;
To His dear Son for sinners given,
   Whose watchful grace we daily prove;
To God the Holy Ghost on high:
   O ever be His comfort nigh,
And teach us, free from sin and fear,
   To please Him here,
And serve Him in the sinless sphere!
Schneesing.

65

1. "JESUS sinners doth receive!"
O may all this saying ponder,
Who in sin's delusions live,
And from God and heaven wander:
This alone sure hope can give —
"Jesus sinners doth receive!"

3. We deserved but grief and shame,
   Yet His words, rich grace revealing,
Pardon, peace, and life proclaim;
   Here their ills have perfect healing

Who with humble hearts believe —
"Jesus sinners doth receive!"

3. Sheep that from the fold did stray
Every faithful shepherd seeketh;
Weary souls that lost their way
Christ the Shepherd seeks and taketh
In His arms, that they may live —
"Jesus sinners doth receive!"

4. Come, ye wanderers, one and all,
Come, ye all have invitation;
Come, obey His gracious call,
Come and take His free salvation;
Come, this cheerful word believe —
"Jesus sinners doth receive!"

5. I, a sinner, come to Thee,
Lord, relieve me of my burden,
Tender mercy show to me,
Saviour, grant to me Thy pardon,
Let this word my soul relieve —
"Jesus sinners doth receive!"

6. Henceforth I need fear no foe;
Though as scarlet my transgression,
It shall be as white as snow
By the virtue of Thy passion,

For in this word I believe —
"Jesus sinners doth receive!"

7. Now my conscience is at ease,
Now I fear no condemnation:
Christ, who grants me full release,
Cancels every obligation;
For in faith to Him I cleave —
"Jesus sinners doth receive!"

8. "Jesus sinners doth receive!"
He received me too; hence never
I shall perish, but shall live
With my Lord in heaven forever,
When this sinful world I leave, —
"Jesus sinners doth receive!"

Neumeister.

66

1. LORD, to Thee I make confession,
I have sinned and gone astray,
I have multiplied transgression,
Chosen for myself my way.
Forced at last to see my errors,
Lord, I tremble at Thy terrors.

2. But from Thee how can I hide me,
   Thou, O God, art everywhere;
   Refuge from Thee is denied me
   Or by land or sea or air;
   Nor death's darkness can enfold me,
   So that Thou shouldst not behold me.

3. Yet though conscience' voice appall me,
   Father, I will seek Thy face;
   Though Thy child I dare not call me,
   Yet receive me to Thy grace;
   Do not for my sins forsake me,
   Let not yet Thy wrath o'ertake me.

4. For Thy Son hath suffered for me,
   And His blood He shed for sin;
   That can heal me and restore me,
   Quench this burning fire within;
   'T is alone His cross can vanquish
   These dark fears, and soothe this anguish.

5. Then on Him I cast my burden,
   Sink it in the depths below.
   Let me feel Thy gracious pardon,
   Wash me, make me white as snow.
   Let Thy Spirit leave me never,
   Make me only Thine forever!

John Franck.

67

1. SAVIOUR, when in dust to Thee
Low we bow the trembling knee;
When repentant to the skies
Scarce we lift our weeping eyes;
O by all Thy pains and woe,
Suffered once for man below,
Bending from Thy throne on high, —
Hear our solemn litany.

2. By Thy birth and early years,
By Thy human grief and tears,
By Thy fasting and distress
In the lonely wilderness,
By Thy victory in the hour
Of the subtle tempter's power, —
Jesus, look with pitying eye,
Hear our solemn litany.

3. By Thine hour of dark despair,
By Thine agony of prayer,
By the purple robe of scorn,
By Thy wounds, Thy crown of thorn,
By Thy cross, Thy pangs and cries,
By Thy perfect sacrifice, —
Jesus, look with pitying eye,
Hear our solemn litany.

REPENTANCE.

4. By Thy deep expiring groan,
By the sealed sepulchral stone,
By Thy triumph o'er the grave,
By Thy power from death to save, —
Mighty God, ascended Lord,
To Thy throne in heaven restored,
Prince and Saviour, hear our cry,
Hear our solemn litany.

Sir Robert Grant.

XIII. Faith and Justification.

68

1. DEAR Christian people, now rejoice,
And banish all your sadness,
While with united heart and voice
We sing with love and gladness,
And tell how God beheld our need,
And wrought that sweet and wondrous deed
That hath so dearly cost Him.

1. Fast bound in Satan's chains I lay,
Death brooded darkly o'er me,
My sins oppressed me night and day,
Therein my mother bore me,

And always deeper still I fell,
In all my life was nothing well,
So sore had sin possessed me.

3. My good works could avail me naught,
For they with sin were stained,
My will against God's justice fought,
And dead to good remained;
My anguish drove me to despair,
Whilst death frowned on me everywhere,
And hell yawned just before me.

4. But God from all eternity
Looked on me in compassion;
His tender mercy flowed tow'rd me,
He willed my souls salvation;
His father's heart yearned over me:
What greater love than this could be,
Which gave His richest treasure?

5. He spake to His beloved Son:
" 'T is time to take compassion;
Go Thou, my Son, my heart's bright Crown,
And bring to man salvation;
From sin and sorrow set him free,
Slay bitter death for him, that he
May live with Thee forever."

6. The Son delighted to obey,
    And, born of virgin mother,
    Awhile in this low world did stay,
    And thus became my brother;
    His mighty power He hidden bore,
    A servant's form like mine He wore,
    My foe for me to vanquish.

7. To me He spake: "Hold fast by me,
    I am thy Rock and Castle,
    Myself I wholly give for thee,
    For thee I strive and wrestle;
    For I am thine, and thou art mine,
    Henceforth my place is also thine,
    The foe shall never part us.

8. "I know that he will shed my blood,
    And of my life bereave me,
    But I will bear it for thy good;
    Be steadfast and believe me:
    My life from death the victory wins,
    My innocence doth bear thy sins,
    And thus thou art delivered.

9. "And when to heaven I ascend,
    My glory to inherit,
    I still will be thy Lord, and send

To thee my Holy Spirit,
To comfort thee in every woe,
Instruct thee how me right to know,
And into truth to guide thee.

10. "As I have done and taught, so thou
To do and teach endeavor;
Then shall my kingdom flourish now,
And God be praised forever;
And this last counsel give I thee:
From men's additions keep thou free
The treasure I have left thee."

Luther.

69

1. NOW I have found the ground wherein
Sure my soul's anchor may remain;
The wounds of Jesus, for my sin
Before the world's foundation slain;
Whose mercy shall unshaken stay,
When heaven and earth are fled away.

2. Father, Thine everlasting grace
Our feeble thought surpasses far;
Thy heart still melts with tenderness,
Thine arms of love still open are,

Returning sinners to receive,
That mercy they may taste, and live.

3. O Love, thou bottomless abyss!
My sins are swallowed up in Thee:
Covered is my unrighteousness,
No spot of guilt remains on me;
While Jesus' blood, through earth and skies,
Mercy — free, boundless mercy — cries.

4. With faith I plunge me in this sea,
Here is my hope, my joy, my rest;
Hither, when hell assails, I flee,
I look into my Saviour's breast:
Away, sad doubt and anxious fear!
Mercy is all that's written there.

5. Though waves and storms go o'er my head,
Though strength, and health, and friends be gone;
Though joys be withered all and dead,
Though every comfort be withdrawn:
On this my steadfast soul relies,
Father, Thy mercy never dies.

6. Fixed on this ground will I remain,
Though my heart fail, and strength decay;
This anchor shall my soul sustain,

When earth's foundations melt away,
Mercy's full power I then shall prove,
Loved with an everlasting love.

J. A. Rothe.

70

1. JESUS, Thy blood and righteousness
My beauty are, my glorious dress;
'Midst flaming worlds, in these arrayed,
With joy shall I lift up my head.

2. When from the dust of death I rise,
To take my mansion in the skies,
Even then shall this be all my plea:
"Jesus hath lived and died for me."

3. Bold shall I stand in that great day,
For who aught to my charge shall lay?
Fully through Thee absolved I am
From sin and fear, from guilt and shame.

4. This spotless robe the same appears,
When ruined nature sinks in years;
No age can change its glorious hue
The robe of Christ is ever new.

5. And when the dead shall hear Thy voice,
Thy banished children shall rejoice;

Their beauty this, their glorious dress, —
Jesus, Thy blood and righteousness.

Zinzendorf.

71

1. ROCK of ages, cleft for me,
Let me hide myself in Thee!
Let the water and the blood
From Thy riven side which flowed,
Be of sin the perfect cure,
Save me, Lord, and make me pure!

2. Not the labors of my hands
Can fulfil Thy law's demands;
Could my zeal no respite know,
Could my tears forever flow, —
All for sin could not atone:
Thou must save, and Thou alone.

3. Nothing in my hand I bring,
Simply to Thy cross I cling;
Naked, come to Thee for dress;
Helpless, look to Thee for grace;
Foul, I to the Fountain fly;
Wash me, Saviour, or I die!

4. While I draw this fleeting breath,
When mine eyelids close in death,

When I soar to worlds unknown,
See Thee on Thy judgment throne,—
Rock of ages, cleft for me,
Let me hide myself in Thee!

Toplady.

72

1. JUST as I am without one plea,
   But that Thy blood was shed for me,
   And that Thou bidst me come to Thee,
      O Lamb of God, I come.

2. Just as I am, and waiting not
   To rid my soul of one dark blot,
   To Thee, whose blood can cleanse each spot,
      O Lamb of God, I come.

3. Just as I am, though tossed about
   With many a conflict, many a doubt,
   Fightings and fears within, without,
      O Lamb of God, I come.

4. Just as I am, poor, wretched, blind;
   Sight, riches, healing of the mind,
   Yea, all I need in Thee to find,
      O Lamb of God, I come.

5 Just as I am: Thou wilt receive,
   Wilt welcome, pardon, cleanse, relieve;
   Because Thy promise I believe,
     O Lamb of God, I come.

6. Just as I am; Thy love unknown
   Has broken every barrier down;
   Now to be Thine, yea, Thine alone,
     O Lamb of God, I come.
                              Ch. Elliott.

XIV. Praise to Jesus.

73

1. JESUS! the very thought is sweet;
   In that dear name all heart-joys meet:
   But oh! than honey sweeter far
   The glimpses of His presence are.

2. No word is sung more sweet than this,
   No sound is heard more full of bliss,
   No thought brings sweeter comfort nigh,
   Than Jesus, Son of God most High.

3. Jesus, the hope of souls forlorn,
   How good to them for sin that mourn!

To them that seek Thee, oh how kind!
But what art Thou to them that find?

4. No tongue of mortal can express,
No pen can write the blessedness;
He only who hath proved it knows
What bliss of love from Jesus flows.

5. O Jesus, King of wondrous might!
O Victor, glorious from the fight!
Sweetnes that may not be expressed,
And altogether loveliest.

6. Abide with us, O Lord, for aye,
Fulfil us with Thy grace, we pray;
And with Thine own true sweetness feed
Our souls, from sin and darkness freed.

Bernard of Clairvaux.

74

1. JESUS, Jesus, nought but Jesus
Shall be e'er my wish and zeal;
Now I form the resolution
That, as Jesus wills, I will,
For my heart, which He hath filled,
Ever cries: Lord, as Thou wilt.

2 E'er 't is He for whom I'm living,
  Whom I'm loving faithfully;
  He it is to whom I'm giving
  What in love He gave to me,
  His dear blood hides all my guilt.
  Lead Thy child, Lord, as Thou wilt.

3. Seems e'er aught to be a treasure,
  Which offensive is to Thee.
  Oh, then take away such pleasure,
  Real blessings give to me.
  Let my heart with Thee be filled;
  Take myself, Lord, as Thou wilt.

4. Unto death let me endeavor
  Thee to please in good and ill;
  In me, through me, with me ever,
  Lord accomplish Thy good will,
  Let me die, on Thee, Lord, built.
  When, and where, and as Thou wilt.

5. Saviour, I will sing Thy praises,
  For Thou unto me didst bring
  Thine own self and all Thy graces,
  That I joyfully may sing: —
  Be it unto me, my shield,
  As Thou wilt, Lord, as Thou wilt.

Ludaemilia Elisabeth, Countess,
of Schwarzburg

75

1. JESUS, priceless treasure,
Source of purest pleasure,
Truest friend to me;
Long my heart hath panted
Till it well-nigh fainted,
Thirsting after Thee.
Thine I am, O spotless Lamb,
I will suffer nought to hide Thee,
Ask for nought beside Thee.

2. In Thine arms I rest me,
Foes who would molest me
Cannot reach me here;
Though the earth be shaking,
Every heart be quaking,
Jesus calms my fear;
Sin and hell in conflict fell
With their heaviest storms assail me,
Jesus will not fail me.

3. Satan, I defy thee;
Death, I need not fly thee;
Fear, I bid thee cease!
Rage, O world, thy noises

Cannot drown our voices
Singing still of peace;
For God's power Guards every hour;
Earth and all the depths adore Him,
Silent bow before Him.

4. Wealth, I will not heed thee,
Wherefore should I need thee,
Jesus is my joy;
Honors, ye may glisten,
But I will not listen,
Ye the soul destroy;
Want or loss Or shame or cross
Ne'er to leave my Lord shall move me,
Since He deigns to love me.

5. Farewell, thou who choosest
Earth, and heaven refusest,
Thou wilt tempt in vain:
Hence, ye sins, nor blind me,
Get ye far behind me,
Come not forth again:
Past your hour, O pomp and power;
Godless life, thy bonds I sever,
Leave thee now for ever!

6. Hence, all thoughts of sadness,
   For the Lord of gladness,
   Jesus enters in;
   Those who love the Father,
   Though the storms may gather,
   Still have peace within;
   Yea, whate'er I here must bear,
   Thou art still my purest pleasure,
   Jesus, priceless treasure!

   John Franck.

76

1. O MORNING-STAR! how fair and brigh'
   Thou beamest forth in truth and light!
   O Sovereign meek and lowly!
   Thou Root of Jesse, David's Son,
   My King and Bridegroom, Thou hast won
   My heart to love Thee solely!
       Lovely art Thou,
   Fair and glorious, All victorious,
       Rich in bl ssing,
   Rule and might o'er all possessing.

2. O King high-born, Pearl dearly won,
   True Son of God and Mary's Son,
   Crown of exceeding glory!
   My heart's Delight I call Thee, Lord,

Pure milk and honey is Thy word,
Thy sweetest gospel story.
    Rose of Sharon,
Hail! Hosanna! Heavenly Manna,
    Feed us ever;
Lord, I can forget Thee never.

3. Clear Jasper, Ruby fervent red,
Deep, deep into my heart do shed
Thy love's bright flame forever;
Fill me with joy, grant me to be
Thy member closely joined to Thee,
Which nought from Thee may sever;
    Toward Thee longing
Doth possess me, Come and bless me,
    For Thy gladness
Eye and heart here pine in sadness.

4. But when Thou look'st on me in love,
There straightway falls from God above
A ray of purest pleasure;
Thy word and spirit, flesh and blood
Refresh my soul with heavenly food,
Thou art my hidden treasure.
    Let Thy Grace, Lord,

Warm and cheer me, O draw near me;
    Thou hast taught us
Thee to seek, since Thou hast sought us

5. Lord God, my Father, mighty shield,
Thou in Thy Son art all revealed,
As Thou hast loved and known me;
Thy Son hath me with Him betrothed,
In His own whitest raiment clothed,
He for His bride will own me.
    Hallelujah!
Life in heaven Hath He given;
    With Him dwelling,
Still shall I His praise be telling.

6. Then touch the chords of harp and lute,
Let no sweet music now be mute,
But joyously resounding;
Tell of the marriage-feast, the bride,
The heavenly Bridegroom at her side,
Of love and joy abounding;
    Shout for Triumph,
Loudly sing ye, Praises bring ye,
    Fall before Him,
King of kings, let all adore Him!

7. Here rests my heart, and holds this fast,
My Love He is the First and Last,
The End and the Beginning;
I welcome death, for I shall rise
Through Him to His own Paradise
Above all tears, all sinning.
  Amen! Amen!
Come, Lord Jesus, Soon release us;
 With deep yearning,
Lord, we look for Thy returning.

Nicolai.

77

1. THE Lord my pasture shall prepare,
And feed me with a shepherd's care;
His presence shall my wants supply,
And guard me with a watchful eye;
My noonday walks He shall attend,
And all my midnight hours defend.

2. When in the sultry glebe I faint,
Or on the thirsty mountain pant;
To fertile vales and dewy meads
My weary wandering steps He leads,
Where peaceful rivers, soft and slow,
Amid the verdant landscape flow.

3. Though in a bare and rugged way,
   Through devious, lonely wilds I stray,
   Thy bounty shall my pains beguile;
   The barren wildernes shall smile,
   With sudden greens and herbage crowned,
   And streams shall murmur all around.

4. Though in the paths of death I tread,
   With gloomy horrors overspread,
   My steadfast heart shall fear no ill,
   For Thou, O Lord, art with me still;
   Thy friendly crook shall give me aid,
   And guide me through the dreadful shade.
   Joseph Addison.

78

1. JESUS is the Name we treasure,
   Name beyond what words can tell;
   Name of gladness, Name of pleasure,
   Ear and heart delighting well;
   Name of sweetness passing measure,
   Saving us from sin and hell.

2. 'Tis the Name for adoration,
   Name for songs of victory,
   Name for holy meditation
   In this vale of misery,

Name for joyful veneration
By the citizens on high.

3. 'Tis the Name that whoso preacheth
Speaks like music to the ear;
Who in prayer this Name beseecheth
Sweetest comfort findeth near;
Who its perfect wisdom reacheth
Heavenly joy possesseth here.

4. Jesus is the Name exalted
Over every other name;
In this Name, whene'er assaulted,
We can put our foes to shame;
Strength to them who else had halted,
Eyes to blind, and feet to lame.

5. Therefore we in love adoring
This most blessed Name revere,
Holy Jesus, thee imploring
So to write it in us here,
That hereafter heavenward soaring
We may sing with angels there.

Gloriosi Salvatoris. — Neale.

XV. The Christian Life.

79

1. O GOD, Thou faithful God,
   Thou fountain ever flowing,
   Without whom nothing is,
   All perfect gifts bestowing;
   A pure and healthy frame
   O give me, and within
   A conscience free from blame,
   A soul unhurt by sin.

2. And grant me, Lord, to do,
   With ready heart and willing,
   Whate'er Thou dost command,
   My calling here fulfilling,
   And do it when I ought,
   With all my strength, and bless
   The works I thus have wrought,
   For Thou must give success.

3. Ne'er let me promise aught,
   But I can keep it truly;
   Restrain all idle words,
   And guard my lips e'er duly;

And grant, when in my place
I must and ought to speak,
My words due power and grace,
Nor let me wound the weak.

4. If dangers gather round,
Still keep me calm and fearless;
Help me to bear the cross,
When life is dark and cheerless;
To overcome my foe
With words and actions kind;
When counsel I would know,
Good counsel let me find.

5. With all men let me be
In peace and friendship living,
As far as Christians may.
And if Thou aught art giving
Of wealth and honors fair,
O this refuse me not,
That nought be mingled there
Of goods unjustly got.

6. And if a longer life
Be here on earth decreed me,
And Thou through many a strife
To age at last wilt lead me,

Thy patience in me shed,
Avert all sin and shame,
And crown my hoary head
With pure, untarnished fame

7. Let nothing that may chance
Me from my Saviour sever;
And when I die, Lord, take
My soul to Thee for ever,
And let my body have
A little space, to sleep
Beside a Christian's grave,
And friends that o'er it weep.

8. And when the Day is come,
And all the dead are waking,
O reach me down Thy hand,
Thyself my slumbers breaking;
Then let me hear Thy voice,
And change this earthly frame,
And bid me aye rejoice
With those who love Thy name.

J. Heerman.

80

1. LORD, all my heart is fixed on Thee,
I pray Thee, be not far from me,
With tender grace uphold me.

The whole wide world delights me not,
Of heaven or earth desire I nought,
If but Thy love enfold me.
Yea, though my heart be like to break,
Thou art my trust that nought can shake,
My portion and my hidden joy,
Whose cross did all my bonds destroy;
    Lord Jesus Christ!
My God and Lord! My God and Lord!
Forsake me not who trust Thy word!

2. Rich are Thy gifts! 't was God that gave
My body, soul, and all I have
In this poor life of labor;
O grant that I may through Thy grace
Use all my powers to show Thy praise,
And serve and help my neighbor;
From doctrine false preserve me, Lord;
All lies and malice from me ward;
In every cross uphold Thou me,
That I may bear it patiently;
    Lord Jesus Christ!
My Lord and God! My Lord and God!
In death Thy comfort still afford.

3. O Lord, let Thy dear angels come
In my last hour, to bear me home,
That I may die unfearing;
And in its narrow chamber keep
My body safe in painless sleep
Until my Lord's appearing;
And then from death awaken me,
That these mine eyes with joy may see,
O Son of God, Thy glorious face,
My Saviour, and my Fount of grace!
    Lord Jesus Christ!
Receive my prayer, Receive my prayer;
Thy love I will for aye declare.
Schalling.

81

1. O GOD of Jacob, by whose hand
Thy people still are fed;
Who through this weary pilgrimage
Hast all our Fathers led.

2. To Thee our humble vows we raise,
To Thee address our prayer;
And in Thy kind and faithful breast
Deposit all our care.

3. Through each perplexing path of life
   Our wandering footsteps guide;
   Give us by day our daily bread,
   And raiment fit provide.

4. O spread Thy covering wings around,
   Till all our wanderings cease;
   and at our Father's loved abode
   Our souls arrive in peace.

5. To Thee, as to our covenant God,
   We'll our whole selves resign;
   And thankful own that all we are,
   And all we have, is Thine.
   Doddridge.

82

1. MY GOD and Father, while I stray
   Far from my home on life's rough way,
   O teach me from my heart to say,
   Thy will be done!

2. Though dark my path, and sad my lot,
   Let me be still, and murmur not,
   Or breathe the prayer divinely taught,
   Thy will be done!

3. What though in lonely grief I sigh
   For friends beloved, no longer nigh?
   Submissive would I still reply,
      Thy will be done!

4. If thou shouldst call me to resign
   What I most prize, — it ne'er was mine;
   I only yield Thee what is Thine:
      Thy will be done!

5. Should grief or sickness waste away
   My life in premature decay,
   My Father, I will strive to say,
      Thy will be done!

6. Let but my fainting heart be blessed
   With Thy sweet Spirit for its guest,
   My God, to Thee I leave the rest:
      Thy will be done!

7. Renew my will from day to day,
   Blend it with Thine, and take away
   All that now makes it hard to say,
      Thy will be done!

8. Then, when on earth I breathe no more
   The prayer, oft mixed with tears before,
   I'll sing upon a happier shore,
      Thy will be done!   Charlotte Elliott.

83

1. DEAREST Lord, we come to Thee
Ignorant, but Thou wilt teach us.
We are poor, but graciously
With Thy gifts Thou wilt enrich us.

2. We are weak, but Thou, O Lord,
Mercifully wilt defend us,
And we know it from Thy word,
That Thy Spirit Thou wilt send us.

3. Be our Shepherd good! O may
We obey Thy voice forever!
Dark and dangerous is our way:
Guide Thou us to life's blest river!

From the Danish.

XVI. Morning.

84

1. GOD who madest earth and heaven,
Father, Son, and Holy Ghost,
Who the day and night hast given,
Sun and moon and starry host,
Thou whose mighty hand sustains
Earth and all that she contains.

2. Praise to Thee my soul shall render,
   Who this night hast guarded me;
   My omnipotent defender,
   Who from ill dost set me free, —
   Free from danger, anguish, woe,
   Free from the infernal foe.

3. Let the night of my transgression
   With night's darkness pass away·
   Jesus, into Thy possession
   I resign myself to-day.
   In Thy wounds I find relief
   From my greatest sin and grief.

4. Grant that I may rise this morning
   From the lethargy of sin;
   So my soul, through Thy adorning,
   Shall be glorious within,
   And when breaks Thy judgment day
   I shall not be cast away.

5. Let my life and conversation
   Be directed by Thy word;
   Lord, Thy constant preservation
   To Thy erring child afford.
   Nowhere but alone in Thee
   From all harm can I be free.

6. Wholly to Thy blest protection
   I commit my heart and mind.
   Mighty God to Thy direction
   Wholly may I be resigned.
   Lord, my shield, my light divine,
   O accept, and own me Thine.

7. Lord, to me Thine angel sending,
   Keep me from the subtle foe;
   From his craft and might defending,
   Never let Thy wanderer go,
   Till my final rest be come,
   And Thy angel bear me home.

   AlbertL.

85

1. AWAKE, my soul, and with the sun
   Thy daily stage of duty run;
   Shake off dull sloth, and joyful rise,
   To pay thy morning sacrifice.

2. All praise to Thee who safe hast kept
   And hast refreshed me while I slept:
   Grant, Lord, when I from death shall wake,
   I may of endless life partake.

3. Lord, I my vows to Thee renew;
   Disperse my sins as morning dew;

Guard my first springs of thought and will,
And with Thyself my spirit fill.

4. Direct, control, suggest, this day,
All I design, or do, or say;
That all my powers, with all their might,
In Thy sole glory may unite.

Ken.

86

1. CHRIST, whose glory fills the skies
Christ, the true, the only Light,
Sun of righteousness, arise,
Triumph o'er the shades of night:
Day-spring from on high, be near;
Day-star, in my heart appear.

2. Dark and cheerless is the morn,
Unaccompanied by Thee,
Joyless is the day's return,
Till Thy mercy's beams I see:
Till Thou inward light impart,
Glad my eyes, and warm my heart.

3. Visit then this soul of mine;
Pierce the gloom of sin and grief;
Fill me, Radiancy divine;

Scatter all my unbelief:
More and more Thyself display,
Shining to the perfect day.

C. Wesley.

87

1. LORD, for the mercies of this night
My humble thanks I pay,
And unto Thee I dedicate
The first fruits of the day.

2. Let this day praise Thee, O my God,
And so let all my days:
And O, let my eternal day
Be Thy eternal praise.

John Mason.

XVII. Evening.

88

1. NOW rest beneath night's shadows
Man, beast, wood, town, and meadows,
The world in slumber lies.
But thou, my heart, awake thee,
To fervent prayer betake thee,
Let praise to thy Creator rise.

2. O Sun, where art thou vanished!
   The night thy reign hath banished,
   The foe of day, dark night.
   Farewell; a brighter glory
   My Jesus sheddeth o'er me,
   He fills my heart with joy and light.

3. The day has now departed,
   The golden stars have started
   From out the heaven's blue dome:
   Thus, thus shall I be standing,
   When God shall call, commanding
   To leave this vale of tears and gloom.

4. To rest the body hasteth;
   Its garments off it casteth —
   Types of mortality;
   These I put off, and ponder
   How Christ shall give me yonder
   A robe of glorious majesty.

5. Head, hands, feet are contented,
   For night their work has ended,
   And bids sweet rest begin.
   Swell thou, my heart, with gladness;
   Thou shalt be free from sadness
   Of earth, and from the toil of sin.

6. Ye weary limbs, now rest you,
For toil hath sore oppressed you,
And quiet sleep you crave.
The day and hour is near you
When other hands shall bear you
To rest in your last bed, the grave.

7. My heavy eyes are closing,
In dreamy sleep reposing,
Who shall protect me then?
I to Thy grace betake me,
In danger ne'er forsake me,
O Eye that watchest over men!

8. Lord Jesus, Thou dost love me;
O spread thy wings above me,
And shield me from alarm;
When Satan would devour me,
Let angels then sing o'er me,
"This child of God shall meet no harm!"

9, My loved ones, rest securely,
For God this night will surely
From perils guard your heads;
Sweet slumbers may He send you,
And bid His hosts attend you,
And golden-armed watch o'er your beds.

P. Gerhardt.

89

1. NOW God be with us, for the night is closing;
The light and darkness are of his disposing,
And 'neath His shadow here to rest we yield us,
   For He will shield us.

2. Let evil thoughts and spirits flee before us;
Till morning cometh, watch, O Master, o'er us;
In soul and body Thou from harm defend us;
   Thine angels send us!

3. Let holy thoughts be ours when sleep o'ertakes us,
Our earliest thoughts be Thine when morning wakes us;
All day serve Thee, in all that we are doing
   Thy praise pursuing.

4. As Thy beloved, soothe the sick and weeping
Bid Thou the prisoner lose his griefs in sleeping:
Widows and orphans, we to Thee commend them,
   Do Thou befriend them.

5. We have no refuge, none on earth to aid us,
Save Thee, O Father, who Thine own hast made us;

> But Thy dear presence will not leave them lonely,
>> Who seek Thee only.

6. Father, Thy name be praised, Thy kingdom given,
Thy will be done on earth as 'tis in heaven;
Give daily bread, forgive our sins, deliver
Us now and ever.—Amen.
Bohemian Brethren.

90

1. ABIDE with me! fast falls the eventide;
The darkness deepens: Lord, with me abide!
When other helpers fail, and comforts flee,
Help of the helpless, O abide with me!

2. Swift to its close ebbs out life's little day;
Earth's joys grow dim, its glories pass away;
Change and decay in all around I see;
O Thou who changest not, abide with me?

3. Not a brief glance I beg, a passing word,
But as Thou dwell'st with Thy disciples, Lord,
Familiar, condescending, patient, free,
Come, not to sojourn, but abide with me!

4. Come not in terrors as the King of kings,
    But kind and good, with healing on Thy
              wings:
    Tears for all woes, a heart for every plea;
    O Friend of sinners, thus abide with me!

5. Thou on my head in early youth didst smile,
    And, though rebellious and perverse mean-
              while,
    Thou hast not left me, oft as I left Thee:
    On to the close, O Lord, abide with me!

6. I need Thy presence every passing hour;
    What but Thy grace can foil the tempter's
              power?
    Who like Thyself my guide and stay can be?
    Through cloud and sunshine, O abide with
              me!

7. I fear no foe, with Thee at hand to bless;
    Ills have no weight, and tears no bitterness.
    Where is death's sting? where, grave, thy
              victory?
    I triumph still, if Thou abide with me!

8. Hold Thou Thy Cross before my closing eyes,
    Shine through the gloom, and point me to
              the skies;

EVENING.

Heaven's morning breaks, and earth's vain
 shadows flee;
In life, in death, O Lord, abide with me!
Henry Francis Lyte.

91

1. THROUGH the day Thy love has spared us,
Now we lay us down to rest;
Through the silent watches guard us,
Let no foe our peace molest:
Jesus, Thou our guardian be;
Sweet it is to trust in Thee.

2. Pilgrims here on earth, and strangers,
Dwelling in the midst of foes,
Us and ours preserve from dangers;
In Thine arms may we repose;
And when life's sad day is past,
Rest with Thee in heaven at last.
Thomas Kelly.

92

1. GOD that madest earth and heaven,
 Darkness and light;
Who the day for toil hast given,
 For rest the night;
May Thine angel guards defend us,

Slumber sweet Thy mercy send us,
Holy dreams and hopes attend us
   This livelong night.

2. Guard us waking, guard us sleeping,
   And when we die,
Let us in Thy mighty keeping
   All peaceful lie.
When the trumpet's call shall wake us,
Do not Thou, blest Lord, forsake us,
But to reign in glory take us
   With Thee on high
Heber.

XVIII. Praise and Thanksgiving.

93

1. PRAISE to the Lord, the Almighty, the King
                    of creation!
O my soul, praise Him, for He is thy health
                    and salvation!
   All ye who hear,
Now to his Temple draw near,
Join me in glad adoration!

2. Praise to the Lord, who o'er all things so
wondrously reigneth,
Shelters thee under His wings, yea, so gently
sustaineth;
Hast thou not seen
How thy desires all have been
Granted in what He ordaineth?

3. Praise to the Lord, who hath fearfully, wondrously made thee,
Health hath vouchsafed, and, when heedlessly
falling, hath stayed Thee;
Fainting and weak,
When not a word thou couldst speak,
Wings of His mercy did shade thee.

4. Praise to the Lord, who doth prosper thy
work and defend thee;
Surely, His goodness and mercy here daily
attend thee;
Ponder anew,
What the Almighty can do,
If with His love He befriend thee!

5. Praise to the Lord! O let all that is in me
adore Him!
All that hath life and breath, come now with
praises before Him!

Let the Amen
Sound from His people again,
Gladly for aye we adore Him!

J. Neander.

94

1. SING praise to God who reigns above,
The God of all creation,
The God of power, the God of love,
The God of our salvation.
With healing balm my soul he fills,
And every raging tempest stills;
To God all praise and glory!

2. The angel host, O King of kings,
Thy praise forever telling,
In earth and sky all living things,
Beneath Thy shadow dwelling,
Adore the wisdom which could span,
And power, which formed creation's plan;
To God all praise and glory!

3. What God's almighty power hath made,
His gracious mercy keepeth;
By morning glow or evening shade
His watchful eye ne'er sleepeth;

Within the kingdom of His might,
Lo, all is just, and all is right;
To God all praise and glory!

4. I cried to God in my distress,
His mercy heard me calling;
My Saviour saw my helplessness,
And kept my feet from falling;
For this, Lord, praise and thanks to Thee!
Praise God most High, praise God with me!
To God all praise and glory!

5. The Lord is never far away,
Forsakes His people never,
He is their refuge and their stay,
Their peace and trust forever;
And with a mother's watchful love,
He guides them, wheresoe'er they rove:
To God all praise and glory!

6. When every earthly hope has flown
From sorrow's sons and daughters,
Our Father, from His heavenly throne,
Beholds the troubled waters,
And at His word the storm is stayed
Which made His children's hearts afraid:
To God all praise and glory!

7. Thus all my gladsome way along,
   I'll sing aloud Thy praises,
   That men may hear the grateful song
   My voice unwearied raises:
   Be joyful in the Lord, my heart!
   Both soul and body, bear your part;
   To God all praise and glory!

8. Ye who confess Christ's holy name,
   To God our Lord give glory!
   Ye who the Father's power proclaim,
   To God our Lord, give glory!
   All idols under foot be trod:
   The Lord is God, the Lord is God!
   To God all praise and glory!

9. Then come before His presence now,
   And banish all your sadness;
   Unto the Most High pay your vow,
   And sing with joy and gladness:
   Though sorrow great our soul befell,
   The Lord our God did all things well:
   To God all praise and glory!

Schuetz.

95

1. NOW thank we all our God
   With heart and hands and voices.
   Who wondrous things hath done,
   In whom His world rejoices;
   Who from our mothers' arms
   Hath blessed us on our way
   With countless gifts of love,
   And still is ours to-day.

2. O may this bounteous God
   Through all our life be near us,
   With ever joyful hearts
   And blessed peace to cheer us;
   And keep us in His grace,
   And guide us when perplexed,
   And free us from all ills
   In this world and the next.

3. All praise and thanks to God
   The Father now be given,
   The Son, and Him who reigns
   With them in highest heaven,
   The one eternal God,
   Whom earth and heaven adore;
   For thus it was, is now,
   And shall be evermore.

Rinkart.

96

1. IN GRATEFUL songs your voices raise,
   All people here below,
   To Him whom angels ever praise,
   In heaven His glory show.

2. With gladsome songs now fill the air
   To God, our chiefest joy,
   Who worketh wonders everywhere,
   Whose hands great things employ;

3. Who from our birth to latest years
   Upholds the life He gave;
   Who, when no help from man appears,
   Himself appears to save;

4. Who, though our sin His heart oft grieves,
   Long-suffering grace still shows,
   Remits the pain, our guilt forgives,
   And every good bestows.

5. O may He fill our hearts with cheer,
   Our minds from sorrow keep,
   And cast all care, pain, grief, and fear
   Into the ocean deep.

6. Upon His own loved Israel
   His peace forever rest!

Our toil His bounty prosper well!
May all by Him be blessed.

7. His loving kindness toward us flow
In bounteous streams each day,
And every anxious care we know
Be chased by Him away.

8. As long as here on earth we dwell,
Our Saviour may He be,
Our portion, 'mid death's terrors fell,
To all eternity.

9. And when in death our hearts shall break,
O may He close our eyes,
And let us to new life awake
In mansions of the skies.

P. Gerhardt.

97

1. MY SOUL, now praise Thy Maker!
Let all within me bless His name,
Who maketh thee partaker
Of mercies more than thou dar'st claim.
Forget Him not, whose meekness
Still bears with all thy sin;
Who healeth all thy weakness,
Renews thy life within;

Whose grace and care are endless,
Who saved thee through the past,
And leaves no sufferer friendless,
But rights the wronged at last.

2. He shows to man His treasure
Of judgment, truth, and righteousness,
His love beyond all measure,
His yearning pity o'er distress;
Nor treats us as we merit,
But lays His anger by,
The humble contrite spirit
Finds His compassions nigh;
And high as heaven above us,
As break from close of day,
So far, since He doth love us,
He puts our sins away.

3. For as a tender Father
Hath pity on his children here,
He in His arms doth gather
All who are His in childlike fear;
He knows how frail our powers,
Who but from dust are made,
We flourish as the flowers,
· And even so we fade;
A storm but o'er them passes,

And all their bloom is o'er,
We wither like the grasses,
Our place knows us no more.

4. God's grace alone endureth,
And children's children yet shall prove,
How He with strength assureth
The hearts of all that seek His love.
In heaven is fixed His dwelling,
His rule is over all;
Angels, in might excelling,
Bright hosts, before Him fall.
Praise Him who ever reigneth,
All ye who hear His word,
Nor our poor hymns disdaineth;
My soul, O praise the Lord!

Graumann.

98

1. BEFORE Jehovah's awful throne,
Ye nations, bow with sacred joy:
Know that the Lord is God alone;
He can create, and He destroy.

2. His sovereign power, without our aid,
Made us of clay, and formed us men;
And when like wandering sheep we strayed,
He brought us to His fold again.

3. We are His people, we His care,
Our souls and all our mortal frame:
What lasting honors shall we rear,
Almighty Maker, to Thy name?

4. We'll crowd Thy gates with thankful songs,
High as the heavens our voices raise;
And earth with her ten thousand tongues
Shall fill Thy courts with sounding praise.

5. Wide as the world is Thy command,
Vast as eternity Thy love;
Firm as a rock Thy truth must stand,
When rolling years shall cease to move.

Watts.

99

1. MY SOUL, repeat His praise,
Whose mercies are so great;
Whose anger is so slow to raise,
So ready to abate.

2. God will not always chide;
And, when His wrath is felt,
His strokes are fewer than our crimes,
And lighter than our guilt.

3. High as the heavens are raised
   Above the ground we tread,
   So far the riches of His grace
   Our highest thoughts exceed.

4. His power subdues our sins;
   And His forgiving love,
   Far as the east is from the west,
   Doth all our guilt remove.

5. The pity of the Lord
   To those that fear His name
   Is such as tender parents feel;
   He knows our feeble frame.

6. Our days are as the grass,
   Or like the morning flower;
   If one sharp blast sweep o'er the field,
   It withers in an hour.

7. But Thy compassions, Lord,
   To endless years endure;
   And children's children ever find
   Thy words of promise sure.

   Watts.

100

1. WHEN all Thy mercies, O my God,
   My rising soul surveys,
   Transported with the view, I'm lost
   In wonder, love and praise.

2. Ten thousand thousand precious gifts
   My daily thanks employ;
   Nor is the least a cheerful heart
   That tastes those gifts with joy.

3. Through every period of my life
   Thy goodness I'll pursue;
   And after death, in distant worlds,
   The glorious theme renew.

4. When nature fails, and day and night
   Divide Thy works no more,
   My ever grateful heart, O Lord,
   Thy mercy shall adore.

3. Through all eternity to Thee
   A joyful song I'll raise:
   But oh! eternity 's too short
   To utter all Thy praise.

Joseph Addison.

101

1. O PRAISE ye the Lord!
   Praise Him in the height;
   Rejoice in His Word,
   Ye angels of light;
   Ye heavens, adore Him
   By whom ye were made,
   And worship before Him,
   In brightness arrayed.

2. O praise ye the Lord!
   Praise Him upon earth,
   In tuneful accord,
   Ye sons of new birth;
   Praise Him who hath brought you
   His grace from above,
   Praise Him who hath taught you
   To sing of His love.

3. O praise ye the Lord!
   All things that give sound;
   Each jubilant chord,
   Re-echo around;
   Loud organs, His glory
   Forth tell in deep tone,
   And sweet harp, the story
   Of what He hath done.

3. O praise ye the Lord!
   Thanksgiving and song
   To Him be outpoured
   All ages along:
   For love in creation,
   For heaven restored,
   For grace of salvation,
   O praise ye the Lord!

XIX. The Cross and Consolation.

102

1. When in the hour of utmost need
   We know not where to look for aid;
   When days and nights of anxious thought,
   Nor help nor counsel yet have brought;

2. Then this our comfort is alone,
   That we may meet before Thy throne,
   And cry, O faithful God, to Thee
   For rescue from our misery;

3. To Thee may raise our hearts and eyes,
   Repenting sore with bitter sighs,
   And seek Thy pardon for our sin,
   And respite from our griefs within.

4. For Thou hast promised graciously
To hear all those who cry to Thee,
Through Him whose name alone is great,
Our Saviour and our Advocate.

5. And therefore, Lord, we come to-day,
And all our woes before Thee lay;
For tried, forsaken, lo! we stand,
Peril and foes on every hand.

6. Ah, hide not for our sins Thy face;
Absolve us through Thy boundless grace;
Be with us in our anguish still,
Free us at last from every ill.

7. That so with all our hearts we may
Once more our glad thanksgivings pay,
And walk obedient to Thy word,
And now and ever praise Thee, Lord.

Eber.

103

1. IN GOD, my faithful God,
I trust when dark my road;
Though many woes o'ertake me,
Yet He will not forsake me;
His love it is doth send them,
And when 'tis best will end them.

2. My sins assail me sore,
   But I despair no more;
   I build on Christ who loves me,
   From this Rock nothing moves me,
   For I can all surrender
   To Him, my soul's Defender.

3. Though death my portion be,
   Yet death is gain to me,
   And Christ my life for ever,
   From whom no death can sever;
   Come when it may, He'll shield me,
   To Him I wholly yield me.

4. O Jesus Christ, my Lord,
   So meek in deed and word,
   Thou once didst die to save us,
   Because Thou fain wouldst have us
   After this life of sadness
   Heirs of Thy heavenly gladness.

5. Amen, Amen! we say
   With all our heart for aye;
   Guide us while here we wander,
   Till safely landed yonder,
   Then shall we Lord, e'er praise Thee,
   And sing for joy before Thee.

   Weingaertner.

104

1. IF THOU but suffer God to guide thee,
   And hope in Him through all thy ways,
   He'll give thee strength whate'er betide thee,
   And bear thee through the evil days;
   Who trusts in God's unchanging love
   Builds on the Rock that nought can move.

2. What can these anxious cares avail thee,
   These never-ceasing moans and sighs?
   What can it help, if thou bewail thee
   O'er each dark moment as it flies?
   Our cross and trials do but press
   The heavier for our bitterness.

3. Be only still, and wait His leisure
   In cheerful hope, with heart content
   To take whate'er our Father's pleasure
   And all-discerning love hath sent,
   Nor doubt our inmost wants are known
   To Him who chose us for His own.

4. He knows the time for joy, and truly
   Will send it when he sees it meet,
   When He has only tried us throughly,
   And finds us free from all deceit,

Then cometh He all unaware,
And makes us own His loving care.

5. Nor think amid the heat of trial
That God hath cast thee off unheard,
That he whose hopes meet no denial
Must surely be of God preferred;
Time passes, and much change doth bring,
And sets a bound to every thing.

6. All are alike before the Highest;
'Tis easy to our God, we know,
To raise thee up, though low thou liest,
To make the rich man poor and low;
True wonders still by Him are wrought,
Who setteth up and brings to nought.

7. Sing, pray, and keep His ways unswerving,
Do but thine own part faithfully,
And trust His word; though undeserving,
Thou yet shalt find it true for thee;
God never will forsake in need
The heart that trusts in Him indeed.

Neumark.

105

1. WHO puts his trust in God most just
Hath built his house securely;
He who relies on Jesus Christ,

Heaven shall be his most surely.
Then fixed on Thee My trust shall be,
For Thy truth cannot alter;
While mine Thou art,
Not death's worst smart
Shall make my courage falter.

2. Though fiercest foes My course oppose,
A dauntless front I'll show them;
My champion Thou, Lord Christ, art now,
Who soon shalt overthrow them.
And if but Thee I have in me
With Thy good gifts and Spirit,
Nor death nor hell, I know full well,
Shall hurt me, through Thy merit.

3. I rest me here Without a fear;
By Thee shall all be given
That I can need, O Friend indeed,
For this life or for heaven.
O make me true, My heart renew,
My soul and flesh deliver!
Lord, hear my prayer, And in Thy care
Keep me in peace for ever.

Muehlmann.

106

1. WHATE'ER my God ordains is right,
Holy His will abideth;
I will be still, whate'er He doth,
And follow where He guideth.
  He is my God,
   Though dark my road,
He holds me that I shall not fall;
Therefore to Him I leave it all.

2. Whate'er my God ordains is right,
He never will deceive me;
He leads me in the proper path,
I know He will not leave me,
  And take content
   What He hath sent;
His hand will turn my griefs away,
And patiently I wait His day.

3. Whate'er my God ordains is right,
His loving thought attends me;
No poisoned draught the cup can be
That my Physician sends me,
  But healing due;
   For God is true:
On this unfailing truth I build,
And all my heart with hope is filled.

4. Whate'er my God ordains is right;
   My Light, my Life can never
   Desire my ill; then to His care
   I give myself for ever,
      In weal and woe,
      For well I know,
   I once shall see as sunlight clear
   How faithful was my Guardian here.

5. Whate'er my God ordains is right;
   Though now this cup in drinking
   May bitter seem to my faint heart,
   I take it all unshrinking;
      Tears pass away
      with dawn of day,
   Sweet comfort yet shall fill my heart,
   And pain and sorrow all depart.

6. Whate'er my God ordains is right,
   Here shall my stand be taken;
   Though sorrow, want, or death be mine,
   Yet am I not forsaken;
      My Father's care
      Is 'round me there,
   He holds me that I shall not fall,
   And so to Him I leave it all.

Rodigast.

107

1. COMMIT thou all thy griefs
   And ways into His hands,
   To His sure truth and tender care,
   Who earth and heaven commands;
   Who points the clouds their course,
   Whom winds and seas obey,
   He shall direct thy wandering feet,
   He shall prepare thy way.

2. Thou on the Lord rely,
   So safe shalt thou go on;
   Fix on His work thy steadfast eye,
   So shall thy work be done.
   No profit canst thou gain
   By self-consuming care;
   To Him commend thy cause; His ear
   Attends the softest prayer.

3. Thy everlasting truth,
   Father, Thy ceaseless love,
   Sees all Thy children's wants, and knows
   What best for each will prove.
   And whatsoe'er Thou will'st,
   Thou dost, O King of kings,
   What Thy unerring wisdom chose,
   Thy power to being brings.

4. Thou everywhere hast sway,
And all things serve Thy might;
Thy every act pure blessing is,
Thy path unsullied light.
When Thou arisest, Lord,
What shall Thy work withstand?
When all Thy children want Thou giv'st,
Who, who shall stay Thy hand!

5. Give to the winds thy fears,
Hope, and be undismayed;
God hears thy sighs, and counts thy tears,
God shall lift up thy head.
Through waves and clouds and storms
He gently clears thy way;
Wait thou His time, so shall this night
Soon end in joyous day.

6. Still heavy is thy heart?
Still sink thy spirits down?
Cast of the weight, let fear depart,
and every care be gone.
What though thou rulest not?
Yet heaven and earth and hell
Proclaim, God sitteth on the throne,
And ruleth all things well.

7. Leave to His sovereign sway
   To choose and to command,
   So shalt thou wondering own, His way
   How wise, how strong His hand!
   Far, far above thy thought
   His counsel shall appear,
   When fully He the work hath wrought
   That caused thy needless fear.

8. Thou seest our weakness Lord!
   Our hearts are known to Thee:
   O lift Thou up the sinking hand,
   Confirm the feeble knee!
   Let us in life, in death,
   Thy steadfast truth declare,
   And publish with our latest breath
   Thy love and guardian care.
   P. Gerhardt.

108

1. GOD moves in a mysterious way,
   His wonders to perform;
   He plants His footsteps in the sea,
   And rides upon the storm.

2. Deep in unfathomable mines
   Of never-failing skill

He treasures up His bright designs,
And works His sovereign will.

3. Ye fearful saints, fresh courage take;
The clouds ye so much dread
Are big with mercy, and shall break
In blessings on your head.

4. Judge not the Lord by feeble sense,
But trust Him for His grace;
Behind a frowning providence
He hides a smiling face.

5. His purposes will ripen fast,
Unfolding every hour;
The bud may have a bitter taste,
But sweet will be the flower.

6. Blind unbelief is sure to err,
And scan His work in vain;
God is his own interpreter,
And He will make it plain.
W. Cowper.

109

1. O THOU, from whom all goodness flows,
I lift my heart to Thee;
In all my sorrows, conflicts, woes,
Dear Lord, remember me!

2. When on my aching, burdened heart
   My sins lie heavily,
   Thy pardon grant, new peace impart,
   In love remember me!

3. When trials sore obstruct my way,
   And ills I cannot flee,
   O give me strength, Lord, as my day;
   For good remember me!

4. When worn with pain, disease, and grief,
   This feeble body see,
   Grant patience, rest, and kind relief;
   Hear, and remember me!

5. When in the solemn hour of death
   I wait Thy just decree,
   Be this the prayer of my last breath:
   Dear Lord, remember me!

6. And when before Thy throne I stand,
   And lift my soul to Thee,
   Then, with the saints at Thy right hand,
   Dear Lord, remember me!

   Haweis.

110

1. NEARER, my God, to Thee,
    Nearer to Thee!
    E'en though it be a cross
    That raiseth me;
    Still all my song shall be,
    Nearer, my God, to Thee,
        Nearer to Thee!

2. Though, like the wanderer
    The sun gone down,
    Darkness be over me,
    My rest a stone,
    Yet in my dreams I'd be
    Nearer my God, to Thee,
        Nearer to Thee!

3. There let my way appear
    Steps unto heaven:
    All that Thou sendest me
    In mercy given;
    Angels to beckon me
    Nearer, my God, to Thee,
        Nearer to Thee!

4. Then with my waking thoughts
    Bright with Thy praise,

Out of my stony griefs
Bethel I'll raise;
So by my woes to be
Nearer, my God, to Thee,
   Nearer to Thee!

5. Or if on joyful wing
Cleaving the sky,
Sun, moon, and stars forgot,
Upwards I fly;
Still all my song shall be,
Nearer, my God, to Thee,
   Nearer to Thee.

Sarah F. Adams.

XX. Death.

111

1. IN PEACE and joy I now depart,
   It is God's will;
So full of comfort is my heart,
   So calm and still,
As my God hath promised me,
Death is a gentle slumber.

2. This Jesus Christ hath done for me,
    God's only Son,
Whom Thou, Lord, caused mine eyes to see,
    And makest known
That He is alone our life,
Our Help in need and dying.

3. Him hast Thou unto all seth forth,
    In wondrous grace,
And to His kingdom called the earth,
    To share His place,
By Thy precious, wholesome word,
In every place resounding.

4. He is the Hope and saving Light
    That sinners need,
And those who know Thee not aright
    Will teach and lead;
He is Israel's hope and joy,
His people's praise and glory.
                              Luther.

112

1. MY LIFE is hid in Jesus,
And death is gain to me;
Then whensoe'er He pleases,
I meet it willingly.

2. For Christ, my Lord and Brother,
   I leave this world so dim,
   And gladly seek that other
   Where I shall be with Him.

3. My woes are nearly over,
   Though long and dark the road;
   My sin His merits cover,
   And I have peace with God.

4. Then when my powers are failing,
   My breath comes heavily,
   And words are unavailing,
   O hear my sighs to Thee!

5. When mind and thought, O Saviour,
   Are flickering, like a light
   That to and fro doth waver
   Ere 'tis extinguished quite;

6. In that last hour, O grant me
   To slumber soft and still,
   No doubts to vex or haunt me,
   Safe anchored on Thy will;

7. And so to Thee still cleaving
   Through all death's agony,
   To fall asleep believing,
   And wake in heaven with Thee.

8. Amen! Thou Christ, my Saviour,
   Wilt grant this unto me.
   Thy Spirit lead me ever,
   That I fare happily.

   Anna, Countess of Stollberg.

113

1. I FALL asleep in Jesus' wounds,
   There pardon for my sins abounds;
   Yea, His dear blood and righteousness
   My jewels are, my glorious dress,
   Wherein before my God I'll stand,
   When I shall reach the heavenly land.

2. With peace and joy I now depart,
   God's child I am with all my heart;
   I thank thee, Death; thou leadest me
   To that true life where I would be.
   So, cleansed by Christ, I fear not death;
   Lord Jesus, strengthen Thou my faith!

   Eber.

114

1. O LORD, my God, I cry to Thee!
   In my distress Thou helpest me.
   My soul and body I commend

Into Thy hands; Thine angel send,
To guide me home, and cheer my heart,
When Thou shalt call me to depart.

2. O Jesus Christ, Thou Lamb of God,
Once slain to take away our load,
Now let Thy cross, Thine agony
Avail to save and solace me,
Thy death to open heaven, — and there
Bid me the joy of angels share.

3. O holy Spirit, at the end,
Sweet Comforter, be Thou my Friend!
When death and hell assail me sore,
Leave me, O leave me nevermore!
But bear me safely through the strife,
As Thou hast promised, into life!

Selnecker

115

1. WHEN my last hour is close at hand,
And I must hence betake me,
Lord Jesus Christ, beside me stand,
Nor let Thy help forsake me.
To Thee my soul I now commit,
And safely Thou wilt cherish it,
Until again Thou wake me.

2. Conscience will sting my memory sore,
    And guilt my heart encumber;
    Yet though as sands upon the shore
    My sins may be in number,
    I will not quail, but think of Thee,
    Thy death, Thy sorrows, borne for me,
    And sink in peace to slumber.

3. I have been grafted in the Vine,
    And thence my comfort borrow;
    And surely, Thou wilt keep me Thine
    Through utmost pain and sorrow;
    Yea, though I die, I die to Thee,
    Who through Thy death hast won for me
    Heaven's bright eternal morrow.

4. Since Thou from death didst rise again,
    In death Thou wilt not leave me;
    Thy life declares my fears are vain,
    And doubts no more shall grieve me;
    For Thou wilt have me where Thou art,
    And so with joy I can depart,
    And know Thou wilt receive me.

5. And so I stretch my arms to Thee,
    Now, O Lord Jesus, take me!
    Peaceful and calm my sleep shall be,

No human voice shall wake me;
But Thou wilt ope the heavenly door
To life and bliss forevermore,
Thou who dost ne'er forsake me.

N. Heermann.

116

1. FAREWELL I gladly bid thee,
False, evil world farewell!
Thy ways are vain and giddy.
With thee I would not dwell;
In heaven are joys untroubled,
I long for that bright sphere,
Where God rewards them doubled
Who served Him truly here.

2. Do with me as it pleases
Thy heart, O Son of God;
When anguish on me seizes,
Help me to bear my load;
Nor do my sorrows lengthen,
But take me hence on high:
My fearful spirit strengthen,
And let me calmly die.

3. When all around is darkling,
Thy name and cross, still bright,

Deep in my heart are sparklin
Like stars in blackest night.
Appear Thou in Thy sorrow, —
For Thine was woe indeed, —
And from Thy cross I borrow
All comfort heart can need.

4. Thou diedst for me, — O hide me
When tempests round me roll;
Through all my foes O guide me,
Receive my trembling soul.
If I but grasp Thee firmer,
What matters pain when past?
Hath he a cause to murmur
Who reaches heaven at last?

5. O write my name, I pray Thee
Now in the Book of Life;
So let me here obey Thee,
And there, where joys are rife,
Forever live before Thee,
Thy perfect freedom prove,
And tell, as I adore Thee,
How faithful was Thy love.

Herberger.

117

1. Who knows how near my end may be?
   Time speeds away, and death comes on;
   How swiftly, ah! how suddenly
   May death be here, and life be gone!
   My God, for Jesus' sake I pray
   Thy peace may bless my dying day.

2. The world that smiled when morn was come
   May change for me ere close of eve;
   So long as earth is still my home
   In peril of my death I live;
   My God, for Jesus' sake I pray
   Thy peace may bless my dying day.

3. Teach me to ponder oft my end,
   And, ere the hour of death appears,
   To cast my soul on Christ, its friend,
   Nor spare repentant sighs and tears;
   My God, for Jesus' sake I pray
   Thy peace may bless my dying day.

4. And let me now so order all,
   That ever ready I may be
   To say with joy, whate'er befall,
   Lord, as Thou wilt, so lead Thou me;
   My God, for Jesus' sake I pray
   Thy peace may bless my dying day.

5. Let heaven to me be ever sweet.
   And this world bitter let me find;
   That I 'mid all its toil and heat
   May keep eternity in mind;
   My God, for Jesus' sake I pray
   Thy peace may bless my dying day.

6. O Father, cover all my sins
   With Jesus' merits, who alone
   The pardon that I covet wins,
   And makes his long-sought rest my own;
   My God, for Jesus' sake I pray
   Thy peace may bless my dying day

7. His sorrows and His cross I know
   Make death-beds soft, and light the grave,
   They comfort in the hour of woe,
   They give me all I fain would have;
   My God, for Jesus' sake I pray
   Thy peace may bless my dying day.

8. From Him can naught my soul divide,
   Nor life nor death can part us now;
   I thrust my hand into His side,
   And say, My Lord and God art Thou!
   My God, for Jesus' sake I pray
   Thy peace may bless my dying day.

9. In holy Baptism long ago
   I joined me to the living Vine;
   Thou lovest me in Him I know,
   In Him Thou dost accept me Thine;
   My God, for Jesus' sake I pray
   Thy peace may bless my dying day,

10. And I have eaten of His flesh,
    And drunk His blood, — nor can I be
    Forsaken now, nor doubt afresh,
    I am in Him, and He in me;
    My God, for Jesus sake I pray
    Thy peace may bless my dying day.

11. Then death may come, or tarry yet,
    I know in Christ I perish not,
    He never will His own forget,
    He gives me robes without a spot;
    My God, for Jesus' sake I pray
    Thy peace may bless my dying day.

12. And thus I live in God at peace,
    And die without a thought of fear,
    Content to take what God decrees,
    For through His Son my faith is clear;
    His grace shall be in death my stay,
    And peace shall bless my dying day.

Emilie Juliana, Countess of
Schwarzburg-Rudolstadt.

118

1. I WOULD not live alway; I ask not to stay
Where storm after storm rises dark o'er the way;
The few lurid mornings that dawn on us here
Are enough for life's woes, full enough for its cheer.

2. I would not live alway, thus fettered by sin,
Temptation without, and corruption within:
E'en the rapture of pardon is mingled with fears,
And the cup of thanksgiving with penitent tears.

3. I would not live alway; no, welcome the tomb!
Since Jesus hath lain there, I dread not its gloom;
There sweet be my rest, till He bid me arise,
To hail Him in triumph descending the skies.

4. Who, who would live alway, away from his God?
Away from yon heaven, that blissful abode,
Where the rivers of pleasure flow o'er the bright plains,
And the noontide of glory eternally reigns?

5. Where the saints of all ages in harmony meet,
    Their Saviour and brethren transported to greet;
    While the songs of salvation eternally roll,
    And the smile of the Lord is the feast of the soul!

    Wm. Aug. Muhlenberg.

XXI. Burial.

119

1 NOW LAY we calmly in the grave
   This form, whereof no doubt we have
   That it shall rise again that day,
   In glorious triumph o'er decay.

2. To earth again we here entrust
   What from dust came, and turns to dust.
   And from the dust again shall rise,
   When God's own trumpet fills the skies.

3. His soul forever lives in God,
   Whose grace his pardon hath bestowed,
   Who through His Son redeemed him here
   From bondage unto sin and fear.

4. His trials and his griefs are past,
   A blessed end is his at last;
   Christ's yoke he bore, and did His will,
   And though he died he liveth still.

5. His soul lives free from grief and care,
   The body sleep's calm rest shall share,
   Till God shall Death himself destroy,
   And raise it into glorious joy.

6. He suffered pain and grief below,
   Christ heals him now from all his woe;
   For him hath endless joy begun;
   He shines in glory like the sun.

7. Then let us leave him to his rest,
   And homeward turn; for he is blest.
   And we must well our souls prepare,
   When death shall come, to meet him there.

9. So help us, Christ, our Hope in loss!
   Thou hast redeemed us by Thy cross
   From endless death and misery:
   We praise, we bless, we worship Thee!

M. Weisse.

120

1. O HOW BLEST are ye beyond our telling
   Who have passed through death, with God are dwelling,
   For ever risen
   From the troubles of our earthly prison.

2. Here, as in a dungeon, grief hath bound us,
   Cares and fears and terrors still surround us;
   Our best endeavor
   But in toil and heart-ache issues ever;

3. While that ye are in your mansions resting,
   Safe and free at last from all molesting
   No pain or sighing
   There may break the rest you are enjoying.

4. Christ doth wipe away all tears and crying,
   Ye possess what we must seek with sighing;
   To you are chanted
   Songs that ne'er to mortal ears were granted.

5. O who would not for that realm of gladness
   Fain forsake this world of grief and sadness?
   Who loves delaying
   In a land of shadows and decaying?

6. Come, we pray Thee, from our post release us,
Quickly guide us to Thy heaven, Lord Jesus:
   In Thee our spirit
Can alone true joy and rest inherit.

Dach.

121

1. SET BOUNDS to thy sorrow and grieving,
And seek in God's word thy relieving;
Let mourning not grow into sinning;
This dying is true life's beginning.

2. Bound up in its shroud, amidst weeping,
This corpse is laid down to its sleeping,
Let emblems of sleep be the token,
That one day death's bonds shall be broken.

3. Although now the heart no more beateth,
The eye with thine own never meeteth,
God's sleeping ones are not forsaken;
From slumber He'll bid them awaken.

4. This body, so wasted and shattered,
This dust that 'midst dust shall be scattered,
Shall then be raised up, and inherit
New life with the glorified spirits.

5. The grain sown to-day in the furrow,
No trace leaves behind it to-morrow,

Yet lo, soon the fresh blade is springing,
Glad cheer to the husbandman bringing!

6. O Earth, we lay down in thy bosom
A seed from which life once shall blossom;
Receive it in charge of its Maker:
'Tis therefore we call thee God's acre.

7. A soul in this frame was residing
That trustfully followed Christ's guiding,
And now sees unveiled the salvation
It hoped for with glad expectation.

8. This body — O Earth, thou must shield it;
Now to thy safe keeping we yield it,
Till Christ comes again, to awake it
And like to His body to make it.

9. We praise Thee and thank Thee, O Father,
That Thou Thine own children dost gather
To sleep aft·r life's fitful story;
From sleep, to the mansions of glory.

Prudentius.

122

1. ASLEEP in Jesus! blessed sleep,
From which none ever wakes to weep:
A calm and undisturbed repose,
Unbroken by the last af foes.

2. Asleep in Jesus? O how sweet
   To be for such a slumber meet;
   With holy confidence to sing
   That Death has lost his venomed sting!

3. Asleep in Jesus! peaceful rest,
   Whose waking is supremely blest:
   No fear, no woe shall dim that hour
   That manifests the Saviour's power.

4. Asleep in Jesus! O, for me
   May such a blissful refuge be:
   Securely shall my ashes lie,
   And wait the summons from on high.
          Mackay.

123

1. HARK! a voice, it cries from heaven,
   Happy in the Lord who die:
   Happy they to whom 'tis given,
   From a world of grief to fly!
   They indeed are truly blest;
   From their labors then they rest.

2. All their toils and conflicts over,
   Lo! they dwell with Christ above;
   O! what glories they discover

In the Saviour whom they love!
Now they see Him face to face,
Him who saved them by His grace.

* 'Tis enough, enough for ever,
'Tis His people's bright reward;
They are blest indeed, who never
Shall be absent from their Lord!
O that we may die like those
Who in Jesus then repose!
Thomas Kelly.

124
At the burial of a child.

1. TENDER Shepherd, Thou hast stilled
Now Thy little lamb's brief weeping;
Oh, how peaceful, pale, and mild
In its narrow bed 'tis sleeping,
And no sigh of anguish sore
Heaves that tittle bosom more.

2. In this world of pain and care,
Lord, Thou wouldst no longer leave it;
To Thy meadows bright and fair
Lovingly Thou dost receive it;
Clothed in robes of spotless white
Now it dwells with Thee in light.

3. O Lord Jesus, grant that we
There may live where it is living,
And the blissful pastures see
That its heav'nly food are giving;
Lost awhile our treasured love,
Gained forever safe above.
Meinhold.

XXII. Judgment and Eternity.

125

1. WAKE, awake, for night is flying,
The watchmen on the heights are crying:
Awake, Jerusalem, at last!
Midnight hears the welcome voices,
And at the thrilling cry rejoices:
Come forth, ye virgins, night is past'
The Bridegroom comes, awake!
Your lamps with gladness take!
    Hallelujah!
    With bridal care
    Yourselves prepare,
To meet your Bridegroom; He is near!

2. Zion hears the watchmen singing,
   Her heart with heavenly joy is springing
   She wakes, she rises from her gloom;
   For her Lord comes down all glorious,
   The strong in grace, in truth victorious,
   Her Star is ris'n, her Light is come!
   Ah come, Thou blessed Lord,
   O Jesus, Son of God,
      Hallelujah!
      O grant that we
      In heav'nly glee
   Eat of Thy Supper, Lord, with Thee!

3. Now let all the heavens adore Thee,
   And men and angels sing before Thee,
   With harp and cymbal's clearest tone;
   Of one pearl each shining portal,
   Where we are with the choir immortal
   Of angels round Thy dazzling throne;
   Nor eye hath seen, nor ear
   Hath yet attained to hear
      So much glory;
      Therefore will we
      Eternally
   Sing hymns of joy and praise to Thee!

Nicolai.

126

1. GREAT God, what do I see and hear!
The end of things created!
The Judge of man I see appear,
On clouds of glory seated.
The trumpet sounds, the graves restore
The dead which they contained before;
Prepare, my soul, to meet Him.

2. The dead in Christ shall first arise,
At the last trumpet's sounding;
Caught up to meet Him in the skies,
With joy their Lord surrounding;
No gloomy fears their souls dismay;
His presence sheds eternal day
On those prepared to meet Him.

3. But sinners, filled with guilty fears,
Behold His wrath prevailing,
For they shall rise, and find their tears
And sighs are unavailing;
The day of grace is past and gone;
Trembling they stand before the throne,
All unprepared to meet Him.

4. Great God what do I see and hear!
   The end of things created!
   The Judge of man I see appear,
   On clouds of glory seated!
   Beneath His cross I view the day
   When heaven and earth shall pass away,
   And thus prepare to meet Him.
   From Ringwaldt

127

1. THAT day of wrath, that dreadful day,
   When heaven and earth shall pass away!
   What power shall be the sinner's stay?
   How shall he meet that dreadful day?

2. When shriveling like a parched scroll,
   The flaming heavens together roll;
   When louder yet, and yet more dread,
   Swells the high trump that wakes the dead?

3. Lord, on that day, that wrathful day,
   When man to judgment wakes from clay,
   Be Thou the trembling sinner's stay,
   Though heaven and earth shall pass away.
   Walter Scott.

128

1. DAY of wrath! O day of mourning!
   See fulfilled the prophets' warning,
   Heaven and earth in ashes burning!

2. O what fear man's bosom rendeth,
   When from heaven the Judge descendeth,
   On whose sentence all dependeth!

3. Wondrous sound the trumpet flingeth,
   Through earth's sepulchres it ringeth,
   All before God's throne it bringeth.

4. Death is struck, and nature quaking,
   All creation is awaking,
   To its Judge an answer making

5. Lo! the Book, exactly worded,
   Wherein all hath been recorded;
   Thence shall Judgment be awarded.

6. When the Judge His seat attaineth,
   And each hidden deed arraigneth,
   Nothing unavenged remaineth.

7. What shall I, frail man, be pleading?
   Who for me be interceding,
   When the just are mercy needing?

8. King of majesty tremendous,
   Who dost free salvation send us,
   Fount of pity, then befriend us!

9. Think, kind Jesus! my salvation
   Caused Thy wondrous incarnation;
   Leave me not to reprobation.

10. Faint and weary Thou hast sought me,
    On the cross of suffering bought me; —
    Shall such grace be vainly brought me?

11. Righteous Judge! for sin's pollution
    Grant Thy gift of absolution,
    Ere that day of retribution.

12. Guilty, now I pour my moaning,
    All my shame with anguish owning;
    Spare, O God, Thy suppliant, groaning

13. Thou the sinful Mary saved'st;
    Thou the dying thief forgavest;
    Me Thou also hope vouchsafest.

14. Worthless are my prayers and sighing,
    Yet, good Lord, in grace complying
    Rescue me from fires undying!

15. With Thy favored sheep O place me,
    Nor among the goats abase me,
    But to Thy right hand upraise me!

16. While the wicked are confounded,
    Doomed to flames of woe unbounded,
    Call me with Thy saints surrounded.

17. Low I kneel, with heart-submission,
    Strewn with ashes of contrition;
    Succor Thou my lost condition!

---

18. Day of tears, O day of mourning!
    From the dust of earth returning
    Man for judgment must prepare him:
    Spare O God, in mercy spare him!
    Lord, all-pitying Jesus blest,
    Grant us Thine eternal rest. — Amen.

    Thomas de Celano.

129

1. JERUSALEM, my happy home,
   Name ever dear to me!
   When shall my labors have an end
   In joy, and peace, and Thee?

2. When shall these eyes thy heaven-built walls
   And pearly gates behold?
   Thy bulwarks, with salvation strong,
   And streets of shining gold?

3. O when, thou city of my God,
   Shall I thy courts ascend,
   Where evermore the angels sing,
   Where sabbaths have no end?

4. There happier bowers than Eden's bloom,
   Nor sin nor sorrow know;
   Blest seats! through rude and stormy scenes
   I onward press to you.

5. Why should I shrink at pain and woe,
   Or feel at death dismay?
   I've Canaan's goodly land in view,
   And realms of endless day.

6. Apostles, martyrs, prophets there
   Around my Saviour stand;
   And soon my friends in Christ below
   Will join the glorious band.

7. Jerusalem, my happy home!
   My soul still pants for thee;
   Then shall my labors have an end,
   When I Thy joys shall see.

   Fr. Baker.

130

1. JERUSALEM, thou city fair and high,
   Would God I were in thee!
   My longing heart fain, fain to thee would fly,
   It will not stay with me;
   Far over vale and mountain,
   Far over field and plain,
   It hastes to seek its Fountain,
   And quit this world of pain.

2. O happy day, and yet far happier hour,
   When wilt thou come at last?
   When fearless to my father's love and power,
   Whose promise standeth fast,
   My soul I gladly render,
   For surely will His hand
   Lead her with guidance tender
   To heaven, her fatherland.

3. A moment's space, and gently, wondrously,
   Released from earthly ties,
   The fiery car shall bear her up to thee
   Through all these lower skies,

To yonder shining regions,
While down to meet her come
The blessed angel legions,
And bid her welcome home.

4. O Zion, hail! Bright city, now unfold
The gates of grace to me!
How many a time I longed for thee of old,
Ere yet I was set free
From yon dark life of sadness,
Yon world of shadowy naught,
And God had given gladness,
The heritage I sought.

5. O what array, O what a glorious host
Comes sweeping swiftly down?
The chosen ones on earth who wrought the most,
The Church's brightest crown,
Our Lord hath sent to meet me,
As in the far off years
Their words oft came to greet me
In yonder land of tears.

6. The Patriarchs' and prophets' noble train,
With all Christ's followers true,
Who bore the cross, and patient did sustain
What tyrants dared to do,

I see them shine for ever,
All glorious as the sun,
'Mid light that fadeth never,
Their perfect freedom won.

7. And when within that lovely Paradise
At last I safely dwell,
From out my soul what songs of bliss shall rise!
What joy my lips shall tell,
While happy saints are singing
Hosannas o'er and o'er,
Pure Hallelujahs ringing
Around me evermore.

8. Innumerous choirs before the shining throne
Their joyful anthems raise,
Till heaven's glad halls are echoing with the tone
Of that great hymn of praise,
And all its host rejoices,
And all its blessed throng
Unite their myriad voices
In one eternal song.

Meyfart.

Doxologies.

1.   C. M.
TO FATHER, Son, and Holy Ghost,
The God whom we adore,
Be glory, as it was, is now,
And shall be evermore.

2.   S. M.
TO GOD, the Father, Son,
And Spirit, One in Three,
Be glory, as it was, is now,
And shall for ever be.

3.   L. M.
PRAISE God, from whom all blessings flow;
Praise Him, all creatures here below;
Praise Him above, ye heav'nly host,
Praise Father, Son, and Holy Ghost.

4.   C. P. M.
TO FATHER, Son, and Holy Ghost,
The God whom heaven's triumphant host
And saints on earth adore,
Be glory, as in ages past,
And now it is, and so shall last,
When time shall be no more.

5.   H. M.
   TO GOD the Father, Son,
   And Spirit, ever blest,
   Eternal Three in One,
   All worship be addressed,
     As heretofore It was, is now,
     And shall be so For evermore.

6.   7. 6.
   TO FATHER, Son, and Spirit,
   Eternal One and Three,
   As was, and is for ever,
   All praise and glory be.

7.   7s.
   PRAISE the Name of God most high;
   Praise Him, all below the sky;
   Praise Him, all ye heavenly host,
   Father, Son, and Holy Ghost:
   As through countless ages past,
   Evermore His praise shall last.

8.   8. 7.
   PRAISE the God of all creation;
   Praise the Father's boundless love;
   Praise the Lamb, our Expiation,
   Praise the King, enthroned above;

Praise the Fountain of salvation,
Him by whom our spirits live;
  Universal adoration
  To the one Jehovah give.

9.   8. 7. 7.

GLORY be to God the Father,
Glory be to God the Son,
Glory be to God the Spirit,
Everlasting Three in One:
Thee let heaven and earth adore'
Now, henceforth, and evermore.

10.   11s.

O Father Almighty, to Thee be addressed,
With Christ and the Spirit, one God ever blest,
All glory and worship from earth and from heaven;
As was, and is now, and shall ever be given.

INDEX OF FIRST LINES.

	No.
Abide among us with Thy grace ... (Winkworth*)	6
Abide with me, fast falls the eventide	90
Alas! and did my Saviour bleed	23
All glory be to God on high...... (Winkworth alt.)	1
Almighty God, Thy word is cast	8
A mighty Fortress is our God .... (Th. Carlyle alt.)	45
Asleep in Jesus! blessed sleep	122
Awake, my heart, with gladness....... (Kelly alt.)	29
Awake, my soul, and with the sun	85
Baptized into Thy name most holy....(Winkw. alt.)	59
Before Jehovah's awful throne	98
Blessed Jesus, at Thy word....... (Winkworth alt.)	3
Blessed Jesus, here we stand.....(Winkw. Loy. alt.)	58
Christ, the Lord, is risen to-day	31
Christ, Thou the champion of the band who own. (Winkworth alt.)	49
Christ, whose glory fills the skies	86
Come hither, ye faithful, triumphantly sing	15
Come, Holy Ghost, in faith us teach.(Luth Watch. alt.)	4
Come, Holy Spirit, God and Lord.... (Winkw. alt.)	38

*) The name of the author is, when known, given in the hymn book, below each hymn. The names here added in brackets indicate the translators whose renderings have been adopted; alt. signifies that the translation made use of has has been altered in this collection.

Come, Holy Spirit, heavenly Dove 41
Commit thou all thy griefs .... (J. Wesley) 107

Day of wrath, O day of mourning .... (Jrons. alt) 128
Dear Christian people, now rejoice .... (Winkw. alt.) 68
Dearest Lord, we come to Thee .... (Watchman) 83
Deck thyself, my soul, with gladness .. (Winkw. alt.) 61
Draw us to Thee, Lord Jesus .... (Winkworth) 86

Farewell I gladly bid thee .... (Winkworth alt.) 116
Father of all! whose love profound 44
Fear not, O little flock, the foe .... (Winkworth alt.) 47
From Greenland's icy mountains 52
From heaven above to earth I come ... (Winkw. alt.) 14

God moves in a mysterious way 108
God that madest earth and heaven 92
God who madest earth and heaven .... (Russell) 84
Great God! we sing that mighty hand 18
Great God, what do I see and hear 126

Hark! a voice, it cries from heaven 123
Hail, Thou, once despised Jesus 25
Hail to the Lord's Anointed 11

I fall asleep in Jesus' wounds ..... (Winkworth alt.) 113
If thou but suffer God to guide thee (Winkworth alt.) 104
I know that my Redeemer lives 33
In death's strong grasp the Saviour lay (Winkw. alt.) 28
In God, my faithful God .... (Winkworth alt.) 103
In grateful songs your voices raise ...... (Kelly alt.) 96
In peace and joy I now depart .... (Massie alt.) 111

INDEX OF FIRST LINES. 199

I would not live alway; I ask not to stay..........	118
Jerusalem, my happy home..........................	129
Jerusalem, thou city fair and high....(Winkw. alt.)	130
Jesus Christ, my sure defence........(Winkw. alt.)	30
Jesus Christ, our blessed Saviour.......(Massie alt.)	60
Jesus is the Name we treasure.....................	78
Jesus, Jesus, nought but Jesus..............(Crull)	74
Jesus lives, He bursts the grave.............(Crull)	84
Jesus, O my King and Saviour...............(Crull)	27
Jesus, priceless treasure................(Winkworth)	75
Jesus sinners doth receive.............. (Mills alt.)	65
Jesus! the very thought is sweet...................	73
Jesus Thy blood and righteousness.......(J. Wesley)	70
Just as I am, without one plea	72
Let me be Thine forever..................(Loy alt.)	50
Let us all with gladsome voice........(Winkworth)	13
Lift up your heads, ye mighty gates...(Winkworth)	10
Lord, all my heart is fixed on Thee....(Winkworth)	80
Lord, dismiss us with Thy blessing	9
Lord, for the mercies of this night	87
Lord God, to us fore'er secure ....(Crull)	53
Lord Jesus Christ, be present now... .(Winkw. alt.)	2
Lord Jesus Christ, in Thee alone......(Winkw. alt.)	64
Lord Jesus Christ, with us abide......(Winkw. alt.)	48
Lord, keep us steadfast in Thy word...(Winkw. alt.)	46
Lord, Thou art the Truth and Way...(Church Book)	7
Lord, Thy death and passionn give.... (Winkworth)	22
Lord, to Thee I make confession...... (Winkworth)	66

INDEX OF FIRST LINES.

My God and Father, while I stray	82
My life is hid in Jesus............(Winkworth alt.)	112
My soul, now praise thy Maker....(Winkworth alt.)	97
My soul, repeat His praise........................	99
Nearer, my God, to Thee	110
Now God be with us, for the night is closing(Winkw.)	89
Now I have found the ground wherein.. (J. Wesley)	69
Now lay we calmly in the grave...(Winkworth alt.)	119
Now let us raise our voices .... (Kelly alt.)	17
Now rest beneath night's shadow...(Winkworth alt.)	88
Now thank we all our God........(Winkworth alt.)	95
O bleeding Head and wounded ....(Crull)	21
O Christ, our true and only Light..(Winkworth alt.)	51
O darkest woe. ....(Winkworth alt.)	26
O God of Jacob, by whose hand	81
O God, Thou faithful God............(Winkworth)	79
O Holy Spirit, enter in...........(Winkworth alt.)	40
O how blest are ye beyond our telling (Winkw. alt.)	120
O Lord, how shall I meet Thee....... (Winkw. alt.)	12
O Jesus, dearest Lord, to Thee..............(J. B.)	62
O Lamb of God, most blameless............(Crull)	19
O Lord, God Father, thanks to Thee........ (Crull)	16
O Lord, my God, I cry to Thee.... (Winkworth alt.)	114
O Morning Star, how fair and bright...(Winkworth)	76
O my child fear God the Lord..............(Crull)	54
O Thou, from whom all godness flows.........(alt.)	109
Our Father dear in Heav'n above......(Winkw. alt.)	57
Our Lord is risen from the dead.................	87

INDEX OF FIRST LINES.

Out of the depths I cry to Thee.....Winkworth alt.)	63
Over Cedron Jesus treadeth ....(Jeffrey)	20
O praise ye the Lord.............................	110
Praised be the Lord, my God ....(Crull)	43
Praise to the Lord, the Almighty...(Winkworth alt.)	93
Rock of Ages, cleft for me....	71
Saviour, when in dust to Thee....................	67
Set bounds to thy sorrow and grieving (L. Watch alt.)	121
Since Christ has gone to heaven, His home (Wink. alt.)	35
Sing praise to God who reigns above......(Cox alt.)	94
Tender shepherd, Thou hast stilled.....(Winkworth)	124
That men a godly life might lead..........(Massie)	55
That day of wrath, that dreadful day..............	127
The Lord my pasture shall prepare.................	77
This is the day the Lord hath made...............	5
Thou who art Three in Unity..........(Massie alt.)	42
Through the day Thy love has spared us.....	91
Wake, awake, for night is flying...(Winkworth alt.)	125
We all believe in One true God....(Winkworth alt.)	56
We pray Thee, Lord God, Holy Ghost.. (Massie alt.)	39
Whate'er my God ordains is right. (Winkworth alt.)	106
When all Thy mercies, O my God................	100
When in the hour of utmost need. ...(Winkworth)	102
When I survey the wondrous Cross..............	24
When my last hour is close at hand...(Winkworth)	115
Who is this that comes from Edom..............	32
Who knows how near my end may be (Winkw. alt.)	117
Who puts his trust in God most just....(Winkworth)	105

www.ingramcontent.com/pod-product-compliance
Lightning Source LLC
Chambersburg PA
CBHW020922230426
43666CB00008B/1542